JOYRIDE
A Soulful Journey Along A1A
Florida's Coastal Byway

Copyright © 2024 Becky Magnolia
All rights reserved.

No part of this book may be reproduced or transmitted in any form or by any means, electronic or mechanical, including photocopying, recording, or by any information storage and retrieval system, without written permission of the author, except for the inclusion of brief quotations in a review.

Published by Magnolia Moonrise Publishing
www.BeckyMagnolia.com
October 2024

Front Cover Photo Credit: Heather Hoyt, HKH Photos
Editor: Karin Nicely Lord
Layout and Design: Becky Magnolia
Interior Photographs: Becky Magnolia

Table of Contents

Introduction……………………………………………………………………………7

Part I…………………………………………………………………………………11

Part II………………………………………………………………………………..21

The Virtues of the Dirt-Road District……………………………………………22

    Randy Odom

        Rodie's Place

Sit, Sip, and Forget about the World a Bit………………………………………32

    Jackie & Don Buckingham

        The Flagler Tea Company

Dr. Bob Fends Off Hungry Eels…………………………………………………..44

    Bob Pickering

        Marineland

A Surprise Resurrection……………………………………………………………58

    James Powell

        Ragga Surf Café

Tonic for a Broken Heart………………………………………………………….69

    Denise Hagan

        Raining Wildflowers

Part III………………………………………………………………………………79

This book is dedicated to those who've gone beyond.

I love you, Dad. Thank you.

Kinship Redefined..**80**
    Ayolane Halusky
        Earth Kinship Kayak Tours & Nature Education

I Came Upon a Child of God..**100**
    Tovah Janovski
        Hope in the Wilderness

Golf Cart Escapades...**114**
    Ellen Karp-Bendana
    Surfside Estates

Part IV...**140**

The Writing on the Wall..**144**
    Jeremie Purdy
    Debra Jean's

The Old Roads..**154**
    Wanda Lee & Destini Wilson

Index of Photographs **170**

Hello, and welcome to my little book!

I have spent the past three days trying to write an introduction for you. The manuscript itself is complete, but I sit here frozen, wondering how to welcome you, my new reader-friend, into this book.

When I started this little project, I had no idea the impact it would have on my life. The original assignment I had made for myself was simple: I'd spend one month talking to as many people as I could who live along the twenty-mile stretch of Florida State Road A1A between Flagler Beach and the Matanzas Inlet.

I would conduct interviews with local business owners, take photos, and document my process in journal form. I would then self-publish and perhaps make enough money to cover the cost of my caramel-latte addiction. Simple, right?

But I added one more stipulation to the writing process.

About a week before I started my journey, I watched an interview with musician Frank Zappa. In the video, he discusses his spontaneous performance style. I was riveted. I loved the boldness, the brashness, the fearlessness of getting on a stage and revealing the true you. So that night, not thinking much about it, I casually texted a guy I had just met on a dating app, "I think I'm going to write my next book like an improv jazz performance."

He simply replied, "Cool."

...and for some reason, that sealed the deal.

From that point forward, every event, every thought, every feeling, every reflection that occurred during this month-long adventure, no matter how raw or uncomfortable, was fair game for the book. Spontaneity and curiosity became the name of my game.

What I had forgotten, however, was that when we choose to dive head first into the grand river of life, we sign a kind of contract with the Universe. We, in essence, open our arms out wide, lean back into a cosmic trust fall, and say, "Okay, world, I'm ready to play!"

I know from experience this way of living can be thrilling but not always easy. I find when we play with the Universe, life becomes its own story, its own adventure. Magic happens. But in the game of the cosmic trust fall, things also will sometimes feel rocky and uncomfortable. They will not always go our way, and yet, somehow….

…in some way…

…we get what we need.

Over the course of the month-long process, it became evident that perhaps what we *need* as a collective isn't just another light and friendly travel book but something rich and deep and full of layers, embedded with truth. What we need—what *I* needed—was a true journey…a journey of the soul, one that reveals who we are and heals us to our bones.
As this book project concludes for me, I feel changed. Somehow the heavy grief, the shame, the doubt I have carried, perhaps for my whole life, feels lighter, less weighty. It appears that

this book and these people, who I have randomly chosen to be part of this story, have somehow inadvertently helped me heal.

Traditionally, after a first draft of a book is complete, I will usually go back in to adjust, delete, and update what I had initially written. But in honor of my original Frank Zappa plan, I kept the contents of this one close to the raw documentation of what I recorded each day.

After sitting with a total of twenty different people and working with hours of transcribed material, I have learned that spontaneous human conversation looks very different when written on a page. I worked hard to honor my guests' words and bring you the energy of our conversations—the laughter, the pauses, the reflection. To help with the flow of the book, I chose to omit portions of the conversations and left out several of the interviews in their entirety.

To me, each conversation in this book is alive with wisdom, beauty, and heart. I hope you feel it too.

Thank you for joining me on this crazy, fun, and fanciful road trip. Enjoy the Ride!

In Love and Gratitude,
Becky Magnolia
August 8th, 2024

PART I

"I will let myself be silently drawn by the strange pull of what I truly love."

–Lyrics from "Keep Walking"
by Lindsey Scott

June 10th, 2024

Becky's Journal

I'm sitting in a booth at Bronx House Pizza in the unincorporated town of The Hammock, Florida, writing from my phone. The men beside me in a huge red upholstered booth sip beers while Green Day plays on the speakers.

It's Monday afternoon, and my favorite local café, Debra Jean's, is closed. So rather than beginning my writing journey with a good cup of coffee as I had planned, I'm starting this book here, with a slice of pepperoni pizza.

My plan is to devote the next month to talking with as many people as I can who live and work along A1A, the famous Florida historic and scenic coastal byway. I will be interviewing whoever piques my interest along the way. But before I dive in with the interviews, I want to give you some backstory.

"Don't Make Me Cross the Bridge"

I remember vividly the first time I crossed the bridge into Flagler Beach. Six of us were packed in a minivan, along with our pet bird and enough snacks and entertainment to engage our kids for the twenty-one-hour drive from Wisconsin to Florida.

My husband at the time and I had been hooked on travel shows. One of our favorite shows featured adventurous couples who had relocated with their young families to exotic places.

We had both lived in Madison, Wisconsin, for most of our lives and were itching for something radically different. So in early 2011, in the evenings when the kids were in bed, we'd pull up the Maps app and search the Florida coastline for the perfect future home. I knew I liked St. Augustine, but it wasn't quite right, so I trailed my finger southward along State Road A1A.

In our search, we found a little town about twenty miles north of Daytona called Flagler Beach. Situated along the Atlantic Ocean, it checked all our boxes as far as proximity to the beach and schools.

But in 2011, aside from a handful of realtor pages, there was not a lot of information about this sleepy Florida beach town. We knew little more than what we could gather from a few school and restaurant reviews.

As I continued my rigorous searching, however, I discovered a brief video clip on YouTube featuring a fun-loving hippie gal at an event in Veterans Park. She was a host, beaming with joy, at a food festival.[1]

I remember thinking, "Well, this gal looks happy. I bet this is a cool place to live."

So while the kids and I stayed in Wisconsin, my husband did a solo trip down to this mystery town. From the Beachfront Motel, he texted me, "I think you're going to love it."

That was all I needed. I was ready to take the plunge.

But crossing that bridge over the Intracoastal to Flagler Beach, I didn't have that awestruck reaction most folks do. Just days before, we had packed up our house and stepped away from our former lives. Life was on the cusp of major change.

---

[1] I found out years later that the "fun-loving hippie gal" in the video was none other than Carla Cline, a Flagler Beach celebrity, well known for her slogan "Please Don't Make Me Cross the Bridge" that now adorns bumper stickers across Florida.

My hometown of Madison, a posh, intellectual college town full of cultural activities, exotic restaurants, and lush, green parks, has a distinct liberal feel. After getting married, my now-ex and I eventually moved with our three kids to a bedroom community outside the city limits of Madison. It was a trendy, affluent suburban landscape, with well-paved streets lined with big homes, where I'd hang out with other stay-at-home moms, sip organic coffees, and do lunch at my favorite cafés. In many ways, it was a picture-perfect dream, but something was missing. Secretly, my soul yearned for more.

So there I was in August of 2011, crossing the bridge. As the small town opened up on the horizon with the ocean in clear view, I panicked.

Yes, the water was lovely, and yes, the sky was magnificent, but all my road-weary eyes could see was a rough-looking town, scraggly palm trees, and a downtrodden bar named Poor Walt Lounge. There were no green lawns, no picture-perfect parks. Where would I order pad thai?

I didn't say it out loud, but secretly, inside, I thought, "What have I done?"

If at that moment a fortune teller had told me my fate, I wouldn't have believed her. Little did I know, this small, unassuming part of the world was about to seduce me, shape me, shake me, mold me, and radically change who I was to become.

Welcome to Florida

Florida State Road A1A runs for 338 miles from Jacksonville to Key West, following closely along the barrier islands that hug the coast. For the purpose of this book, I am focusing on the sweet little twenty-mile section of A1A where I roam—my personal stomping grounds between Flagler Beach and the Matanzas Inlet.

Unlike other parts of coastal Florida, this section of A1A still has the feel of Old Florida. The pace is slower. People take time to be present with one another. This unique part of the world honors a relaxed, community-focused way of life that by its very nature reflects the heart of the landscape.

In our neck of the woods, a hammock is not just a bed you lie in while sipping mai tais. Ecologically speaking, a hammock is a natural area made up of big trees and low underbrush that grow beside swamps, rivers, and oceans. In the hammocks of northeastern Florida, you'll find ancient oaks, towering pines, scrubby cabbage palms, and a wild tangle of underbrush. In fact, it's so jungle-like around here that some of the early Tarzan movies in the 1940s were filmed just down the street from where I sit right now. The people here, the true locals, know the land well. With a deep generational history, their lives are an integral part of this magical, mysterious land.

If you want to experience the natural beauty of our local hammock and the neighboring coastal dunes, I suggest a walk along the Mala Compra Greenway Trail. There's no other part of this area that sings to my heart more than this enchanted trail.

Mala Compra Greenway Trail
115 Mala Compra Rd.
Palm Coast, FL 32137

But a lot is changing here. As I write to you now, the neighboring lot, which has been a wild, untamed woods for quite some time, is being cleared to make a parking lot. In the past few decades, big portions of The Hammock and the dunes that connect it to the Atlantic have been replaced with gated communities, golf courses, and resorts, changing the landscape and the faces of the people who reside here.

Although I don't know exactly how this book will look when it is complete, I do have a main objective. I aim to create a book that is written like a love letter in dedication to a place and its people. I write it as a way to honor and preserve a style of living, sharing with anyone who wants to learn about the power of community and connection.

Okay, I've finished my pizza. It's time to start the adventure.

Thrift-Shop Momma

After paying my bill, I drive just a few blocks down from Bronx House Pizza and make a left turn off A1A into a gravel parking lot. In the front yard of the two-story wooden house stands a towering, ten-foot-tall fiberglass flower, greeting guests as they arrive at the Hammock Thrift Shop. I find a parking spot beneath the trees and head towards the front door.

Unassuming and unpretentious, Hammock Thrift Shop exemplifies the essence of small-town life. It's the perfect post-pizza location to launch my story.

At the front counter, Melinda and Tess move about like hummingbirds, adding new stock and ringing up customers. Melinda sees me and smiles brightly.

Melinda's daughter, Summer, is a brilliant and wild tattoo-adorned surfer girl who I befriended at a writers' workshop a decade ago. Although closer in age to my kids than myself, Summer's wild and bold philosophies mirror my own. She is one of my favorite people.

"Well, hey there, Becky," Melinda says. "How've you been, girl? I see on Facebook you've been busy."

Melinda knows I'm always scheming.

"Yeah, I've just started working on a new book. I literally just began writing the first few pages today! It's going to be about A1A and the people who live here."

"Well, I'm sure I could connect you with some people who know the history of The Hammock," she says.

"Actually it's not going to be a history book. I want it to be about the people who live and work here now. I'm starting a list of local business owners who I want to interview."

"Well, that sounds fun," Melinda says, placing a dress back on its hanger.

I wander over to the jewelry case and gaze at the shiny trinkets. We continue to talk.

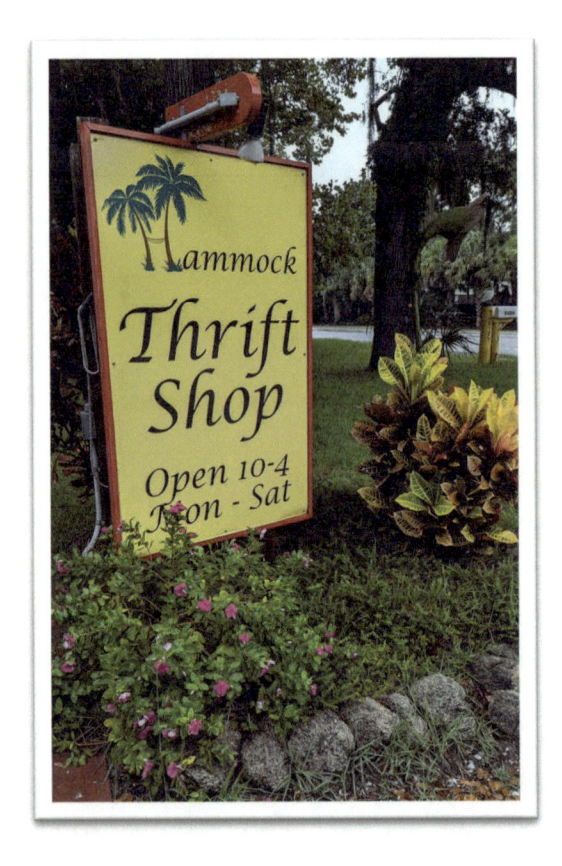

"I saw that you're working up at that new store at the inlet," she says.

I nod with a big smile. "Yup! I'm really enjoying it."

"I'm so glad," she says with her sweet Southern accent. "It's funny, I had just told my husband the other day, 'That Becky needs a job.' You've got too much time on your hands…too much time to think. A job'll be good for you."

I laugh. She isn't wrong. There's nothing like having a sensible Southern momma like Melinda to tell you how she sees it.

Melinda knows I'm a thinker. I like to reflect deeply about…well, everything. It's a double-edged sword as I experience life deeply and intensely. I celebrate it all—both the beauty and the struggle. It makes me poetic, but as she points out, sometimes it's good to get out of my head and into the world.

June 11th, 2024

Becky's Journal

The (Secret) Dancing Queen

I am writing to you this morning from my favorite beach spot. The sun has just risen, and my blanket is spread out wide for me to do my stretches. My favorite music is playing.

About two years ago, I started a solo yoga practice at Jungle Hut Beach Park in The Hammock at sunrise. I'd climb over the temporary fencing marked *No Trespassing* and use the broken walkover as a secret spot where I could stretch, move, and find my center.

But I found holding traditional yoga poses failed to captivate me. I craved motion. I wanted to move my body in just the ways it asked of me. So I bought myself a small Bluetooth speaker, and my daily visits to the broken walkover quickly evolved from static yoga into a full-on spontaneous morning dance.

Now keep in mind I'm no professional dancer. Although I dance, I'm not necessarily good at it. I just love to move. Fortunately, I was there early enough in the morning that I didn't run into a lot of people. However, eventually, the regulars got to know me and would come by to say hi. I ended up pausing often to talk from my perch with the friendly walkers down below.

The dilapidated walkover was eventually replaced. So I traveled further north to find my current morning lookout. I fully realize waking up before the sun and driving down A1A to solo dance at sunrise is not a normal thing to do, but I will tell you, I need this.

This is where I feel most myself, where I move the tight spaces within me, where I get to release the noise in my head and reach into my heart, where I traverse deep down into my belly and awaken the neglected, deeper parts of myself.

I am learning some key lessons as I dance on my perches along A1A. It appears that if we're to live a true, full, and well-rounded life, we must submit to the tides, allow ourselves to merge with the breeze, and surrender to the wild, unpredictable winds that capture us again and again.

Okay, enough about me! I have my first interview in just a few hours.

PART II

"Frankly, there isn't anyone you couldn't love once you've heard their story."

–Mary Lou Kownacki

Randy Odom

Rodie's Place
The Hammock, Florida

The Virtues of the Dirt-Road District

I pull up to Rodie's Place a little after lunch. The small one-story house sits, unassuming, beneath the trees. Out front, a scattering of ten cars are parked in the gravel lot beneath the towering oaks, while a three-foot stuffed black bear dressed in a Hawaiian shirt stands near the hostess station to welcome guests. Owner Randy Odom sits under the covered porch at the end of a long high-top table. He is talking animatedly with a group of regulars he's sharing the table with.

In his bright blue Hawaiian shirt, Randy doesn't strike me as the man in charge. In fact, with his casual demeanor, he appears more like a retired beachgoer who has just stopped by for a beer. But that's part of Randy's charm. It's his low-key attitude that sets the playful, casual vibe for his restaurant.

As I now sit at the long table with Randy and his customers, a waitress named Lisa pokes her head out and asks me about my book project. She brings me a sweet tea, I snap a few photos of the playful crew of regulars, and I begin my interview.

"So how'd you end up in The Hammock?" I ask Randy.

"I was in corporate America for twenty-eight years at IBM," he tells me. "I left there and started my own consulting business. I did that for ten years. But then I said, 'You know what? I'm tired of this. I'm just gonna buy this little two-bedroom house and open up a local breakfast/lunch place.' And here I am."

On July 4th of 2024, Rodie's will be celebrating their five-year anniversary.

"Where'd the name Rodie's come from?" I ask.

"Well, I'm Randy. But Rodie has kind of been like a moniker for me. This place is whatever *Rodie* wants it to be. When someone asks 'How'd you come up with this?' I say, 'I don't know. Rodie came up with it.'"

As the regulars chat amongst themselves, Randy continues, "I wanted this to be a little local place. People come here and they hang out. You get to know the people. You interact with the people. And then, people start to interact with one another, and so it's just like a little hub activity."

I met Randy five years ago, when I was living around the corner on Magnolia Street. At the time, the restaurant was still under construction and Randy was wrestling endlessly with the county about permitting. One day, I came by the restaurant-in-progress to interview him for a story I was writing for the local paper. When Randy explained his grand vision to me as we walked the grounds, the whole thing felt very far off in the distance.

"I'm a sixth-generation Floridian," Randy continues. "I spent thirty years in Minnesota, until my ex-wife gave me the opportunity to..."

He pauses mid-sentence when Lisa, carrying an armful of dishes, leans out from the door and playfully interjects.

"When she gave you an *opportunity* to move back to Florida?"

"Have you heard this before?" he asks with a teasing tone.

"No. Wild guess," she says with a smile and slips back into the restaurant.

Randy goes on:

"My family moved to Fernandina Beach on Amelia Island during World War II. It is, in my opinion, best known for being both Old Florida and New Florida. The Hammock is Old Florida and New Florida together as well."

Randy then explains his theory about The Hammock. According to him, there are two types of communities here, which he categorizes into districts: "the dirt-road districts" and "the compound districts." The dirt-road districts, which include Magnolia Street, Shady Lane, Mala Compra Road, and Hernandez Avenue among others, are the roads that feel a little less tame than the other sections of town. Many of these roads have double-wide trailers, unpaved roads, unmanicured lawns, and are still on septic systems.

The gated communities, or what Randy calls "the compounds," were built in the early 1990s and 2000s. These consist of larger HOA-deeded homes built up along the coastline.

Randy explains, "There's two completely different groups of people in the dirt-road district. You could have a two-million-dollar home across the street from a double-wide. [In this area] you don't have to pay HOAs…and as long as you don't hurt anybody else, you're pretty much golden."

He continues, "One day, I was sitting here, and there were probably four million dollars' worth of cars in the parking lot. The least expensive was probably one hundred eighty thousand dollars. And at the same time, we had people who rode up on their bicycles because it's their only mode of transportation.

"Nobody speaks poorly of anybody else. Nobody looks down on anybody else. You know, it's just kind of a hodgepodge." He pauses and gestures to his staff. "That's one of the reasons why I hired as many Hammockians as I could."

"Is a Hammockian a Hammock resident?" I ask over the din of local diners.

"A Hammockian (pronounced Ham-oak-ian) is more than just a Hammock resident. Probably the best example of Hammockians would be up at Hammock Hardware. They're Hammockians. Hammockians have been here for generations. They're used to the area. They grew up here."

He adds, "I'm now considered a Hammockian because I've been here for twelve years. I've had the business, so I'm a Hammockian."

Randy notes that many people in the gated communities choose to isolate themselves. They opt to not wander outside "the compounds." However, there's another group of compound residents, including some of his customers, who do it differently.

"You have those who adventure out a little bit," he tells me. "They have conversations with people who have different life experiences, and they get to know them. So it's just kind of a nice mixture."

Randy interrupts himself to address Joey and Robin, two regulars, who are talking loudly beside us.

"Hey, you're gonna have to pipe it down a little. I'm doing an interview, " he says in playful jest.

Joey, who I had just met, nods and smiles. "Okay, Randy, we'll use our indoor voices."

Another regular walking by smiles mischievously, leans over to me, and says out of the corner of his mouth, "Talk to me after the interview. I'll tell you the *real* story."

The table laughs.

As the group is talking, Randy stands up and heads into the restaurant. He returns holding a small pink t-shirt on a hanger.

"This is our motto," he says and then reads proudly: "Livin' the Dream in The Hammock."

"Now put it on and model it for her, Randy," says Robin. Robin makes her living selling her handmade jewelry at local farmers' markets all the way from Palm Coast to St. Augustine. I've known her for years and own several pieces of her jewelry.

"Oh, what an adorable top," I say, getting a closer look at the shirt.

Joey leans over to me and says, "You know what? I'll buy you one."

"I'd love that!" I thank him profusely.

Finishing the interview, I leave Rodie's Place with a new, very cool t-shirt, a few new friends, and a reinvigorated sense of energy. *This* is what life along A1A is all about—community, camaraderie, and a warm local vibe.

I head home and type up my notes.

Rodie's Place
5115 N Ocean Shore Blvd
Palm Coast, FL 32137
(386) 283-4647
www.rodiesplace.com

June 12th, 2024

Becky's Journal

Both Sides of the Fence

I spent the morning at my new job as a clerk at The Inlet Beach and General Store. I first met co-owner Adam Morley ten years ago while he was campaigning for a seat on the Florida House of State Representatives.

The day we met, he was sitting in a dunk tank, being pelted by Flagler Beach locals in Veterans Park. I was impressed by his creative, out-of-the-box tactic for engaging potential voters, getting his name into the community. Since then, Adam has run for the position for four election cycles—and has lost every time. And yet, he perseveres. I have a feeling this year he's going to win.

In his early thirties at the time we met, his hair tied back in a ponytail, he was clearly not your usual candidate. I have since learned his politics attract people on both sides of the fence. As the everyman's candidate, he was–and still is–the most unique political candidate I have ever met.

Adam and his amazing wife, Janine, opened The Inlet Beach and General Store in April of this year, just two months before the date I'm writing this. They also own the historic Genung's Fish Camp along the Matanzas River in Crescent Beach. Multi-talented, and with a passion for community and local connection, the couple are also dance instructors. A few years back, I took a West Coast Swing class from them. Now they're my bosses!

The Inlet Beach and General Store sits along A1A between a series of bridges that connect Marineland with the small beach community of Summer Haven and the Matanzas Inlet. Focusing on snacks, fishing supplies, and local wares, they try to buy locally as much as they can. Their aim is to create a community hub where people can connect with one another. So far, it looks like they're doing just that. I love working behind the counter and chatting with the locals and visitors who come by to pick out their beach supplies.

I'm still in training at the shop, so today Janine continued to teach me the ropes. During a downtime, Janine and I got to know each other better.

Janine is a native Floridian. Growing up, she lived with her family in a single wide-trailer, until her mom had their fifth child. Her dad, who was a carpenter, then purchased a horse-trailer bed and on it built a new home. As more children were born, Janine's dad slowly over the years added more rooms to the house that would soon hold eight children total. From what I've gathered from Janine and her sister Renee, it sounds like a wonderful but also sometimes difficult childhood. The family was often just scraping by. While their dad worked, her mom held down the fort, running the busy, hectic household. Janine dropped out of school when she was sixteen and began working. As she said, "I've always worked. I've never stopped."

"My story is a bit different," I told her with some hesitation. The daughter of a psychiatrist, I was raised to be a good intellectual and attended a prominent Midwestern liberal arts college. I sometimes joke that after graduation, I could write a good thesis paper, speak Mandarin Chinese, and quote Nietzsche, but not do much else. In hindsight, although it was never stated out loud, I suspect it had been my parents' hope for me—as was common with some Jewish parents—to find a good man, stay home, and raise a family.

And I did just that. Right out of college, I fell in love with a kind, stable man and chose the traditional route to stay at home with the kids. I wrote books, volunteered in the schools, and occasionally worked odd jobs, but I never had to work a paying job.

To be honest, I was more than a little embarrassed to tell Janine my story. I'm not always proud of my privileged and somewhat naive upbringing, but Janine listened closely and seemed to accept me just as I was.

At one point as I talked, her eyes lit up and she said, "It's like *Titanic*!"

It took me a second to understand, but I soon realized the connection. She was referring to the way the main character, Rose, snuck down below the ship and fell in love with the more earthy way of life of the working class. I laughed. I didn't mind being compared to the movie's heroine.

As we sat next to each other behind the counter, waiting for the next flow of customers to arrive, we marveled at how even with our radically different upbringings we could connect and celebrate each other, both as moms, living along this beautiful stretch of country.

That night after work, I headed south along A1A eighteen miles to Flagler Beach. I was scheduled to meet up with Jackie Buckingham, owner of the Flagler Tea Company, for my next interview, and I was eager to hang out with her and her husband, Don.

Jackie & Don Buckingham

Flagler Tea Company
Flagler Beach, Florida

Sit, Sip, and Forget about the World a Bit

Just one block west of the Flagler Beach pier on South Central Avenue stands an old single-story storefront painted in bright ocean blues. This centrally located building houses three well-known businesses in the quaint and quiet downtown of Flagler Beach.

On the strip, the center shop is the Gallery of Local Art, known around town as GOLA. To the right of GOLA is a potter's studio and gallery—you'll meet the studio owners later in this interview. However, right now, I'm headed to a tiny shop called The Flagler Tea Company.

Out front sit a few tables and chairs and a big outdoor sectional couch, providing the perfect spot for patrons to relax and embody the shop's company slogan: "Sit, Sip, and Forget about the World a Bit."

I enter the shop and am struck by a swirl of exotic scents. In front of me is a case filled with cupcakes, whoopie pies, and muffins. I realize I haven't had dinner yet and gaze wide-eyed at the case. Trying to resist buying everything remaining in the case, I turn to check out an elegant display of Jackie's handmade soaps. Jackie and her husband, Don, notice me in the store and give me a big hello. They've been expecting me.

While Jackie finishes closing up shop, Don sits poised behind the register in his usual spot, his aromatherapy degree hanging prominently on the wall above his head. Jackie offers me a pastry and a tea and sets up two folding chairs in the middle of the store. I hand her one of my lapel mics and start the recorder. We begin our conversation.

"So tell me what brought you here to Flagler Beach."

"We had a little girl back in 2009, and when she was almost two years old, she came down with an illness when we lived in Virginia. They couldn't quite figure it out.

"We knew from living in Florida before that there are three really good children's hospitals here. My mother-in-law lived in the area, in Ormond, so we were like, 'Okay, let's move down here.'

"My husband at the time had called around to find somebody who could figure out what was going on and found a doctor at Nemours [Children's Hospital] in Orlando, and they said, *'Move now.'* So when we got here and got set up, they told us that our daughter would probably be deaf and blind and need a kidney transplant by the time she was a teenager. This is from the initial diagnosis.

"Later on in life, though, we found out it was something else. She will not be deaf and blind. Now that she's a teenager…she's fifteen…her kidney function is still good."

Jackie then goes on to tell me the history of her business.

"We started out with potpourri at a holiday market in town. We had potpourri that my dad showed us how to make. It could be smelled two blocks down. We had our picture taken for the paper about the 'good-smelling scent shop,' and it wasn't too long after that, that we were doing the 9th Street Market and European Village. We then moved into [this location] and started with just our soaps and body butters and aromatherapy products. In 2018, we added on teas and herbs. In 2020, we added on the gluten-free bakery."

A few customers enter the store as we're talking. To stay out of Jackie's way, Don and I step outside and relax on the couch. Don, who was a bit hesitant to talk, at first, happily takes the mic and continues the interview without her.

"So when you moved here, were you instantly charmed by Flagler Beach?" I ask.

"No," Donald answers point blank. "No. I don't like the ocean."

I laugh.

"I know that sounds odd, but she loves the ocean. I do not. I'm a mountain person. I've loved the mountains forever."

Don continues, "But Flagler? No, Flagler was just Flagler. I wasn't sold on it. It wasn't that it wasn't a nice area…but, I dunno, it kind of grows on you. It really does. I think the people mainly do. You start to get to know people…and it's like everything could be going bad and twenty-five people will step up to try to help you make it good.

"You treat people well, and they treat you incredible. And if they don't treat you incredible, they're probably not from here. Would I want to live anywhere else? Probably not."

"Interesting," I answer with a smile.

"I think that being here is incredible. It's sunny," he says.

"And the ocean breeze is so wonderful," I add. "I mean, we're one block away from the water."

"Yeah, and it's peaceful. That's what I was mainly looking for. And you meet a lot of nice people. You make friends. I don't think you'd want to go anywhere else."

I then ask, "When you started the business, were you nervous?"

"You know, you could be nervous [starting a business] or you could just jump straight in. I'm the type of person that will just jump in. If it works, it works. If it doesn't, we try something else. I'm not a 'what if' person. I'm like, 'Why not? Let's give it a shot.' I don't want to look back on it and say, 'I really wish I would have' or 'What would have happened if I would have just…' Nah, try it out, man. That's about living right there. If it works, it works. And if it doesn't, eh, it don't matter."

"And it's working!" I say.

"Yeah, it's working, but it's still a lot of hard work. It's late nights and really early mornings for her with the baking and just trial and error. And baking at sea level—what a nightmare that is."

As we talk, Jackie closes up the shop and settles on the couch beside her husband. The hot summer air is finally cooling off, and the three of us find ourselves relaxing as our conversation continues.

As we talk, Don tells me that he wasn't initially on board with adding gluten-free products to their tea and soap shop.

"I had tried gluten-free food before, and it was horrible—the cardboard pizzas, the snacks that you get that were just bland or gritty. It's just not something that I would want. That's my mindset. But then Jackie started to develop her own flour blends and started to bake, and gluten-free didn't taste gluten-free! So that changed my mind. But I think what really changed my mind was"—he pauses—"I'll never forget that kid's face. He came in. He was probably about five or six years old. All his siblings were running around. Everyone knew what they were getting, but I could see it in his face. He's like, 'I can't get anything.' He just looked like he was kicking stones."

Don continues, "When Jackie asked him, 'What would you like?' he said, 'Well, I don't know. Can I have anything here?' And she's like, 'You can have *everything* here.'

"He lit up like the sun. I mean, he just beamed and got so excited. He didn't know what to get because he could have everything, and he's never had that experience. That was evidence right there. Whether we made it or not, it was a thing just to make that kid's day."

As we talk, Don Davis, owner of the pottery studio next door, saunters by on the sidewalk.

"Hey, Don!" we call to him. Don Davis and I have known each other for years. We had served together on the Flagler Beach economic task force run by the city when I was still a resident seven years ago. I am currently in a pottery class led by his business partner, Audrey.

"My book is becoming a reality, Don!" I tell him as he steps onto the porch. I had gone to him for writing advice when this book was just a concept in my mind. "Come join us and I'll interview you too!"

"Well, I came on a mission. I just have to grab some stuff in the studio, and I'll be right back," Don D. says in his slow, thoughtful way.

After he steps away, Don Buckingham tells me, "Don is wonderful. He's kind of a local celebrity."

With his white hair pulled back in a ponytail, his starched, blue, button-up shirt, and his slow, articulate way of speaking, Don the potter definitely fits the role of the town's resident artist.

I set Don D. up with a microphone, and he begins to tell us his story.

"Where are you from originally?" I ask him.

"I was born in Jacksonville. We always came down this way. Florida has always been home to me. But for most of my adult life, I had been away, pursuing different things—mostly clay work and education. And I moved back here...not because Flagler Beach is a hotbed of ceramic activity or anything like that. Flagler Beach is a wonderful little town right on the ocean, and there aren't very many like it that I know of. So yeah, that's what got me back here."

The conversation wanders to talk about his studio.

"Audrey and I are partners in the studio. It's small, but I feel *really* fortunate to have stumbled into this. I've had this [experience] in my life where I've moved to places that were kind of sleepy. I could afford to live there, like Asheville [North Carolina] in the mid to late

'70s. Asheville was deserted downtown, and I watched it boom into this art area. I was kind of forced out because rents got so high," he says. "Flagler Beach was an idyllic place that I could actually afford to live [in] and have a decent piece of real estate. I feel like I got here at a very lucky time in my life and in the life of this town."

With the construction of a Margaritaville Hotel just a block away, a multimillion-dollar beach restoration project beginning in just a week, and upcoming plans for rebuilding the hurricane-tattered pier, this small, sleepy town is definitely feeling the influence of change.

Don continues, "I drove down Roberts Road across the bridge, and they're going to outnumber our population on this side [of the bridge] with just those condominiums, apartment buildings, and houses that they're putting in. I don't know if that's good or bad, but I expect to see things growing and becoming somewhat more affluent here, which comes with certain elements that are good and certain elements that are maybe not necessarily so good." He pauses and reflects. "This is like the Florida I knew as a kid."

Don B. interjects, "I've driven the [Florida] coast, and this is one of the last remaining small beach towns I think we're gonna find."

As the four of us talk, the sun begins to slowly descend. The big, puffy clouds that build over the ocean begin turning pink and orange in the sky. The air feels settled and calm. Our conversation continues, pensive, slow, and unrushed. After chatting casually for another half hour, I turn off my mics. As I pack up my equipment, I mention my interview scheduled for tomorrow.

"I'm interviewing Bob Pickering out at Marineland. Do you know him?" I ask Don B.

"Oh yes—Bob…" Don smiles and nods as if he knows something I don't. "He's a great guy. I promise you're going to have a blast."

Flagler Tea Company
208 S Central Ave Unit B, Flagler Beach, FL 32136
(386) 631-3962
www.flaglertea.com

June 18th, 2024

Becky's Journal

Interruption by the Sea

I'm sitting outside Sip and Surf Coffee Company in Flagler Beach with an iced coffee and a breakfast sandwich. The woosh of busy traffic on A1A melds with the ongoing roar of the ocean. Several kids play on a pair of swings that hang from the café's awning out front. The air is surprisingly cool for a mid-June morning.

The strong breeze off the ocean whips my hair as I type these words to you into my phone. I'm quite comfortable, with my legs stretched out along the span of the cushy outdoor loveseat, and I'm marveling at the way my life has brought me here to this exact spot with you, the reader. What perfection it is to be writing by the sea.

However, a woman breaks my peace by talking loudly into her phone on the outside veranda. She speaks with a Northeastern accent that I can't quite place as she tries to talk over the sound of the waves and traffic.

I glance her way, hoping to discreetly point out to her that she's being a bit loud. She steps further from me and talks loudly a few more minutes until she approaches me.

"I'm so sorry about that," she says to me. "I was trying to hear that guy, and then I saw you were here, trying to work."

Any annoyance I initially felt dissolves the moment she apologizes. I am grateful to be seen.

"The funny thing is I didn't even want to be talking to him," she says, laughing, and together we smile in agreement about the annoyance of telemarketers.

"Where are you from?" I ask.

"We're from rural Maryland," she says. Her jet-black hair is pulled back in a ponytail, and her arms are decorated with tattoos.

"We've got a place in Ormond by the Sea. It was my husband's uncle's place before he passed."

I mention that I am working on a book about A1A, and she seems interested.

"What do you like about the area?" I ask.

"Oh…well, to me, this is a *rural* beach." She gestures to the ocean across the street. "You can't get this in Miami."

As we talk, her five-year-old granddaughter runs up to show us the tiny white shell she's just discovered.

"Look, Grandma! It looks like a rose."

Small and perfectly curled, it certainly did look like a rose.

We both admire it. I finish writing this section, say my goodbyes to the kind family, and head out.

Sip and Surf
701 N Ocean Shore Blvd Flagler Beach, FL 32136
(386) 338-3241
www.wakesipsurf.com

Yesterday, outside the pottery studio after finishing my ceramics class, I chatted with visual artist and co-owner of the studio Audrey Scherr. Although I didn't have the mics on at that moment, I'll try my best to honor what she said as it seems to be pertinent to my story.

"In Flagler Beach, we get to be ourselves," she said, her wild red hair slipping from her ponytail, her potter's apron spotted with clay. "We don't need to carry expensive purses or sunglasses. We're just whoever we are! Here, people are real. They're not hiding under layers upon layers of pretense. What you see is what you get."

I'll be honest, this morning when I woke up before pottery class, I felt twisted up with uncomfortable emotions that felt unmanageable. After my divorce six years ago, my life was turned inside out. I went from living in a vivid and active household as a wife and mother to being faced with a new identity as a divorcee who spends a great deal of time alone.

In my prior life, I used to secretly fantasize about being alone, of an identity of being an adventurous single woman who decided her own destiny. But now on my own, living that life I so desperately yearned for, solitude can creep up on me with a vengeance. Although I feel deep gratitude for my life, occasionally I'll find myself swarmed by a sense of disconnection and loneliness. It's then I question my purpose and my value in the world.

My antidote to the shadows arrives when I get out of my personal, tight spaces and engage with the world around me. It's the Matanzas River near my house, the ocean, the woods, and this culture of authenticity that Audrey talks about that have been my saving grace from these feelings of isolation. It's odd. I feel safe and comfortable even with strangers, knowing we're all going through tough stuff, taking turns having bad days, difficult months, hard years, while simultaneously we have a connection, each of us grateful for the space we're in.

Bob Pickering
Marineland, Florida

Dr. Bob Fends Off Hungry Eels

It's Saturday morning. I have just dropped my teenage daughter off at her dad's in Flagler Beach and am now headed north along A1A to Marineland. Today's the big day I finally get to meet the famous "Dr. Bob."

Behind the Marineland boardwalk, the Atlantic Ocean sparkles in the noonday sun. Only a few distant clouds break the sky's pristine blueness. Beachgoers who've set up their personal cabanas in the sand lounge in the shade, while children with their parents play in the shallows at low tide.

Marineland is home to an aquatic park now known as Marineland Dolphin Adventure. The original park was founded in 1938, opening its doors decades before SeaWorld existed. Known as "the world's first oceanarium," the historic area has provided the backdrop for several movies throughout the years. Situated along A1A, Marineland, in its heyday, was a huge tourist attraction where visitors who were traveling down the coast could stay overnight and watch dolphin shows in the park. In 1974 the Whitney Lab for Marine Bioscience joined the park across the street. Today, the tiny town that spans a narrow three miles along the coast boasts a population of *fourteen* people, consisting primarily of scientists who work at the lab.

Even though I have never met Bob in person, I recognize him immediately as he approaches from the south end of the boardwalk. Of medium build, in his late 50s, wearing simple glasses and a t-shirt displaying a retro photo of Marineland, he's walking fast, with a happy bounce. On his head, he wears an original Marineland ball cap from the 1980s. He tells me he has worn it just for the occasion.

Bob and I have known each other on Facebook for years. When I was going through a rough transition six years ago, he invited me to join him and his wife for karaoke night. I didn't take them up on it, but I always remembered the kind-hearted gesture.

Although we have never met in person, upon meeting him, I feel the urge to open my arms wide. We hug with enthusiasm, pull back, and laugh. He starts talking right away.

"The funniest thing just happened to me," he says, slightly out of breath.

"Hold on, hold on," I say. "Let me set up my recorder." I fumble to get my phone out and haphazardly turn the recorder on without setting up the mics.

He begins his first story.

"My entire life is just like a *Doctor Who* episode…I'm a big fan of *Doctor Who*. The Doctor, the main character [of the long-running sci-fi television series], usually shows up just in time to help somebody somewhere." Bob talks fast and loud over the roar of the wind and the ocean waves.

"So I pulled in here, and this poor couple, their motorcycle had tipped over down at the south end of the park, here. No one was hurt. I wound up helping them right their motorcycle and be on their way. This stuff keeps happening to me!"

I laugh.

"I just show up at the right time to help somebody."

"That's so great," I say, taking a quick pause to formally set up my microphones.

"Okay…we're set…" I say. "Let's go back. Tell me who you are."

"So my name is Bob Pickering, and I have lived in Flagler County since November of 1980. And I worked at Marineland of Florida from 1983 to 1994. I currently work for Flagler County Emergency Management, which I've done since 1994 until now. I'm going to be celebrating my thirtieth year there on July 5th. I have a lot of connections to Marineland. It is really important to me.

"When I first moved down here, I was like thirteen or fourteen years old and I loved dolphins. I still love dolphins now, but I got completely *obsessed* with Marineland.

"I was a very shy person. I was not the person that you see today. I was a very shy person, hardly talked to anybody. And of course, just moving here from the Boston area—it was like culture shock. One of the first questions that someone asked me…he was a real friendly kid…but he asked me, 'Are you a Yankee or are you a Rebel?' and I'm like, 'I have no idea what you are talking about.'

"Okay, so here's my first Marineland connection," he says. "Let's go further back. In the 1970s, around 1971, my parents came down to Florida to go to Disney, but we also made a side trip to Daytona Beach. Then we made a day trip to Marineland. So when I was very young, I visited Marineland for the very first time. I actually have photos from that. And so that's my first visit to Marineland. I can barely remember that."

Bob's voice is filled with vibrancy as he talks, and I can't help but feel excited by the positive energy he emits.

"So fast forward to 1980, about ten years later. We moved down here. When we drove down from Massachusetts, the first place we stayed in Florida was at the Marineland Quality Inn Hotel, which is basically right where we're standing right now.

"Right here was a huge eight-story structure. It was kind of pyramid-shaped but flat, and all the rooms were oceanfront. My first night in Florida was probably somewhere along here." He points to the span of the boardwalk. "My first meal I ever had as a Florida resident was at the Dolphin Restaurant, which was right there around that palm grove." He gestures towards a group of scraggly trees near where the Ragga Surf Café food truck now sits.

"County residents could get into Marineland for free, so I found myself, every Thursday after school, hanging out at Marineland. My dad or my mom—mostly my dad—would drive me up here, and I would hang out at Marineland. I would play catch with the dolphins, and I would just wander around and mostly just hang around what was called, then, The Marine Studios at the old oceanariums. So mostly I would just hang out around there. And with all that being said, I was still very, very shy, but I was also beginning to come out of my shell a little bit because I was absolutely obsessed with everything Marineland."

"So were you obsessed with the marine animals or the park itself?" I ask.

"It was both." He continues, "I would be up here every Thursday, and any Marineland brochures, flyers, anything like that—I would procure those and hang them in my bedroom. I had the big triple-jump dolphin poster on my wall. I had all that stuff.

"In high school, I was, you know, a science fiction geek, a weather geek, and all that stuff. My class only had one hundred people in it."

"Which school was that?"

"Flagler-Palm Coast High School. Back then it was grades seven through twelve. There was no middle school yet. But, of course, when you're in a small class and you're the only science geek in the entire school…and everyone else is interested in going to parties and drinking and all that stuff…it was kind of, uh, a little bit of a lonely existence, if you will. I wasn't picked on or anything like that, but I was kind of on my own.

"So when I came to Marineland, my only existence I had ever known was high school. But because I was so obsessed with [Marineland], it finally forced me to break through my shyness, and I started actually talking to some of the people who worked here."

Bob tells me, as a kid, he began building a connection with the employees, including Tommy Devoe, the "jumpmaster" at the time who trained the dolphins. Encouraged by Tommy, Bob applied to Marineland at age sixteen and got his first job. He would soon work his way up from custodian to diver. This noble job as staff diver included wearing the heavy bell helmet underwater and hand feeding the dolphins, fish, eels, and rays and regularly cleaning the almost two hundred underwater portholes. Over the years, Bob took on many jobs at the park. He's collected many good stories.

As we talk, we walk down towards the entrance of the Marineland park and Bob begins to tell me some of his stories.

"In the rectangular oceanarium, I believe in the spring of 1987, the water had been really cool. But all of a sudden, it got warmer and the moray eels got very aggressive. They weren't attacking [the divers who regularly cleaned the portholes], but they wanted the food that we carried. So one of the divers got bit.

"Now, they call these things 'the rattlesnakes of the deep' because they have bacteria on their teeth, so if you get bit by one, you're out of action and you have to go to Shark Care."

"Wait, where do you have to go?" I ask, curious what he means by "shark care."

"You have to go to a medical clinic. Shark Care in St. Augustine was the closest one we had at the time."

I nod and he continues, "So one diver got bit. And then another diver got bit. Then another. And over the course of several days, every diver got bit except for me."

"Wow," I say, riveted by his story.

"Now, here I am, going into the rectangular oceanarium. Every diver is out of commission except for me. So I go down, knowing what everyone else has run into, and I start doing the water show. As soon as I'm in there, the eels are on me. It's like a video game. I'm grabbing fish and feeding them."

Bob moves about as he talks, pretending as if he's in that tank, reaching out and feeding the eels. I laugh as he jumps around.

"I'm spinning around in all different directions. I keep twisting and turning."

Bob dances around, reaching out to the imaginary eels around him.

"There's another eel…and there's another eel!" he says.

As he tells his story, a small crowd visiting from St. Augustine begins to form around us.

"I give them each a piece of fish, and they leave me alone. But I get like halfway through to the deep section, and then one of the big green moray eels wraps around my helmet. I can see this green stripe right through the helmet window, his face right in my face.

"So I reached in and got him a herring or a mackerel. He grabbed it and pulled away with it. Then here comes another one…and here comes another one. I have gloves on my hands, so you do have some protection, but the teeth that they have are like needles. They go right through those gloves if you get bit.

"I am so scared. I am on ultra-red alert. So I get to the north ledge, and there's no eels around me. Everyone is satisfied, but then I come back down to the deep section again. I know my boss is watching. Everyone's watching because I'm the last diver standing now. So I'm feeding the eels, and here they come again. They all converge on me one last time.

"I came out unscathed! I was the only diver cleaning all the ports for several days so the other people could get healed."

The crowd that has assembled around Bob and me asks him a few questions. When they leave, I ask Bob if he has any more stories.

He nods.

"Yes," he says, and I notice he's a bit more somber now. "I had a very sad thing happen." He pauses. "Betty, my favorite dolphin, gave birth to her first baby…I want to say it was 1986. I was still in high school. It was in springtime, and I was the first diver on duty right after she gave birth. So they sent me down into the oceanarium to scoop up the placenta. I had this giant scoop net. There's a picture of me I circulated on Facebook. I'm in the helmet, doing a salute. It's me coming back with the placenta. So I scooped it up and hauled it up and gave it to the lab. About three days later, I come in and the chief diver goes, 'The baby's dead.'

"I was the first diver in, so I had orders to put my suit on right away and recover the baby."

Bob's voice slows down as he recounts this next part.

"So, when…when a baby dolphin passes, a momma tries to make it breathe. So Betty is frantically trying to get this thing to breathe, pushing it to the surface, and she's just totally freaked out. So, now, here I come with the big scoop net, and I'm trying to get this thing from her. No luck. No luck anywhere I go. So this goes on for like twenty minutes."

Bob pauses.

"This next part bothers me…" He begins to get choked up. Slowly, with tears in his eyes, he says, "She came and dropped it at my feet and stared at me through my helmet. I will never forget that as long as I live. One of the announcers saw it happen," Bob says. "And so, I scooped her up and I made for the ladder. And Betty just kind of swam around me. I went up the ladder, pulled the baby up, and unhooked [the divers helmet]. I was in tears. The first thing I said [when I was out of the tank] was, 'She gave it to me.'

"I'll never forget that eye staring at me through the helmet."

"What do you think she was trying to tell you?" I ask, tears in my eyes now as well.

"I think she knew the time had come. I don't know if it happened that way because I was the diver there, or because she had particular trust in me. I don't know.

"Betty liked to play games with me a lot. She liked to play this game called 'shells.' It could be annoying if you're trying to clean windows. She'd come up next to you and drop a shell, and you'd have to catch the shell, and she'll drop it again. It's like playing catch. But it's like, 'Betty, I gotta clean windows,' and then she'd just nudge you, and then *really* nudge you, like 'You *will* play shells with me.' And it's like, 'Okay, okay!'

"But she was always one of my favorite dolphins. Betty is still here today. She is the oldest dolphin they have here now."

"How old is she?"

"I would estimate she's in her mid-50s. I'm fifty-seven years old, so I think her age is about the same as mine."

"Do you think she'd know you if you went in there now?" I ask.

"I've had interactions with her, but sadly, her eyesight's almost gone, so if I were to get into the tank with her, because they can sonar, I don't know if she would recognize me or not because we're talking like forty years ago. I don't understand how their stuff works. And plus, my body has physiologically changed since then.

"But on two occasions…and Marineland has been very kind to me…they've let me have some interactions with Betty. And [during] one of those interactions, she did come up and kind of hang out, so who knows?

"They had me speak here at their eighty-fifth anniversary. There's been some moments [at Marineland] that were scary. There's been some moments that were thrilling and blissfully happy. Some that were sad, heartbreaking…some moments boring, some moments frustrating….some moments that got me very upset. And some moments that were just stunningly beautiful. I've seen some of the coolest thunderstorms I've ever seen in my life here in Marineland as they moved out over the ocean. I've seen waterspouts and some of the most gorgeous rainbows.

"But these are examples of how interwoven Marineland has been in my life. It was the first place I stayed when we moved here to Florida, my first dinner as a Florida resident, and three years later, when I turned sixteen, Marineland would be my first job.

"My first bad crush I ever had on a girl was here at Marineland. All that [dating] stuff was so new to me then, and I was so shy, which, you know, when you're attracted to women and you're super, super shy and afraid of rejection and all that stuff…all that doesn't work well.

"The very first time I danced with a girl was here at Marineland as well. They used to have these epic Christmas parties. This girl named Lynn was one of the dolphin trainers. She said, 'Come here and dance,' and she pulled me onto the dance floor.

"But, you know, the first time I did a top-deck show, the first time I announced, the first time I dove, I felt just an incredible, joyful light of happiness. And then when I had to take Betty's dead baby from her…every bit of these experiences helped me become the person I am today. All of that broke me out of my shell. The scary things, the dangerous things increased my confidence significantly, you know? All of that helped build me to who I am today."

Marineland Dolphin Adventure
9600 N Ocean Shore Blvd
Marineland, FL 32080
(407) 563-4701
www.marineland.net

June 19th, 2024

Becky's Journal

Where Everybody Knows Your Name

Today, I'm at The Java Joint Beachside Grill at the north end of Flagler Beach. The joyful energy here is palpable on this Wednesday morning as the waitresses hustle table to table in time to the retro rock music playing on the speakers. Java Joint is a mom-and-pop diner with views of the Atlantic from every window. I've been coming here for years, using my favorite corner table to work on whatever current projects I have in progress.

I recently heard a piece of wisdom from a spiritual teacher. He said you can tell the emotional health of an area by the sparkle in the locals' eyes. Today, I observe as patrons talk with animation, looking at each other eye to eye and simply celebrating life together. Even the waitresses, who are working intensely, pop around with smiles on their faces. We're all here at this moment, experiencing life in our own ways and simultaneously sharing the space's vibrant energy.

I notice two women at the table next to mine are playfully laughing and teasing one another. We start talking to each other across the tables, and I introduce myself. I mention that I'm working on a book. We chat for a bit longer, and I ask if I can take their picture to include in the journey.

Since I started this project, I've been sharing my book-writing adventures on social media. My followers seem to enjoy my exploits, so I keep them posted on the people I meet as I go. A number of individuals in a group called "Flagler Beach for Friends" have reached out to me, suggesting names of people to interview in the book. I've already lined up a few interviews.

Michelle, a waitress who has been at Java Joint for over three years, overhears me talking to the ladies.

"I'm so excited about your book," she says.

"Yeah, me too! It's a lot of fun," I tell her. "In two months, I start grad school at Jacksonville University," I explain to Michelle. "I'm planning to start a private practice as a psychotherapist. This little book project is my last hurrah before I start school full-time. It's a weird project. Even though it's about positivity, I'm also holding space for the difficult stuff." I pause. "Life can be hard," I say.

"Yeah, it can be hard, man." She nods in agreement. Although Michelle and I have only known each other in the roles of waitress and customer, at the moment we feel like old friends. She says, "When we can find the smiles in our day, it's something worth celebrating."

I agree and head out the door.

Java Joint Beachside Grill
2201 N Ocean Shore Blvd
Flagler Beach, FL 32136
(386) 439-1013
www.javajointfb.com

James Powell
Ragga Surf Cafe
Marineland, Florida

A Surprise Resurrection

I park my car in one of the Marineland lots and wander towards the iconic turquoise bus that sits at the top of the hill. The gray-blue ocean flows majestically behind it. It's a particularly windy day, and patrons who sit beneath the turquoise umbrellas are holding tight to their meals as the wind whips around the encampment.

I see co-owner James, and we hug. I have only known James through the cafe, and yet, the two of us have taken the time on occasion to have numerous deep conversations. James and I find a safe spot out of the wind and begin our interview.

"Okay, so tell me about your café," I say.

"Ragga Surf Café is a family business. It's an ownership team made up of my wife and I, my sister and her husband, my mom and dad, and then some of my best friends who I consider family…and some of my cousins as well. There's ten of us that are the ownership team. We started three years ago.

"My best friend and his wife were living in the blue bus—the iconic blue bus that is Ragga Surf Café. He had customized the living space. When we had the opportunity to be on this land, we were looking for a vehicle and decided that we were going to kick him out of his house and turn his bedroom into a kitchen. And so he moved into another RV, and we started renovating the bus into the food truck that it is now.

"We started with two tables in the parking lot, with a generator, and now we have twenty-five to thirty tables on the oceanside, a second truck, and a surf store. My family owns the surf store as well. So there's three vehicles now on the property, and it's just grown like crazy." He pauses. "I think it's a safe haven for people and a peaceful spot for people to meet up."

"So why are you guys here?" I ask.

"Why? Hmm…my parents started a non-profit in 1997. It's called Inter-United Soccer Club. It started as a soccer club in Central Florida and has actually been reborn here in Palm Coast three years ago, with similar timing to the café opening.

"Our mission statement for the non-profit is 'We believe in the power of friendship.' Friendship is the most powerful thing in this world. So we'll use whatever tools we have at our disposal for the sole purpose of making friends.

"Through that non-profit, we use education, music, and soccer to make friends. We've done cultural exchanges in several countries, including China. I lived most of my twenties in China. I've done a lot of cultural exchanges through that non-profit in Peru as well. We also started a non-profit school in Kenya with one of our close friends who got out of poverty and chose to dive back in to raise her community with hope. And we thought there was no better way [to do that] than to start a school. So we helped her start a school there.

"We have a team going there with the mayor of Marineland to try to start an aquaponics farm at the school so the kids can have a sustainable food source and maybe even a sustainable business for their local community.

"The café is just another arm of that. It's a separate business that is not a non-profit, but the heartbeat is the same.

"We make the best food possible because we want to treat our friends with the best food. Our staff…we're all best friends because we believe it has to start together on the bus where we cook together.

"If we love each other, then that will spread out to whoever comes as well. In training, we say to new employees, 'If you feel like you need to talk to somebody for an extra five minutes, don't worry; we'll get the cooking down. Let's take the time to make a friend because that's our main purpose to be here—not just to run a successful business, but to make a friend.'"

I tell James, "One of my big words in life that I keep coming back to in all my projects is *connection*. What does connection mean to you?" I ask.

"Connection is one of my words too," James says. "I think, by the time I'm fifty, I want to be a counselor or life coach, but I want to have the life experience of being fifty before offering that professionally to others."

I smile to myself as he says this. James doesn't know that in one short month, at the age of fifty-two, I'll be returning to school to do just that. I had always wanted to be a counselor, but it wasn't until this year that I fully felt ready.

"I've done self-work to identify what I personally value the most," James says. "It comes down to two words: *expression* and *intimacy*. Intimacy is interchangeable with connection."

James, like me, appreciates deep human connection. He explains, "Oftentimes, we'll try and make a shallow connection [with each other] because it feels good in the moment. It's because we're so thirsty for it. But if we go deeper into the love of it—the patient connection, the kind and the long-suffering of serving somebody—that is what connection means to me."

James tells a story.

"My sister and wife, they run five businesses together. They're the reason for us looking good out here. All the visuals, all the marketing happens through those two powerhouses. And they work without talking, essentially. It's almost like they have the same brain.

"My sister was an art teacher. One of her star students wanted to work for her company. It was her dream job, so my sister took her on as an apprentice. Five years later, she became the VP of the company called Ragamuffin, which is our surf shop. It also had an offshoot called Ragga Wedding."

James pauses and becomes a bit more somber.

"A few days after she was named VP, she died." He speaks slowly. "Our community here is very close. My sister was an art teacher. I was a music teacher. My brother-in-law is a music teacher. My dad was dean of students and an athletic director. My aunt was a teacher. We all worked at the same school in Central Florida. And so, half of the staff [at the café] were our students who've moved over here with us. We're all really close. We've done life together. So it was devastating for our community to lose her.

"She lived with a pacemaker, and so she lived with anxiety over death. She died at twenty-five when the pacemaker just stopped working one morning."

As I listen, I'm feeling his words close to my heart. I pause and reflect on one of my most tender moments coming to Ragga Surf Café. Two years ago, my friend Sky was sick with stage-four cancer. She was new to the area, and although quite weak, she was still mobile. So one day, I decided to bring her up to Ragga. I already knew of its healing power.

At the time, Sky was visibly not well. She was thin, bald from the chemo, and walked with a cane. While café patrons milled about, James had taken the time to talk with her. He had pulled out a traditional Chinese tea set from the back of the bus and served us tea in a traditional Chinese tea ceremony.

As James and I are talking, I reflect with him about the topic of suffering and wonder out loud if sometimes suffering is necessary in order for us to feel the preciousness of life. "Our friend's boyfriend, after she had died, was mourning," James tells me. "Yet he was seeing clearly, maybe for the first time in his life. He said something that was exactly like what you said."

James continues, "I had asked him, 'What is the meaning of this?' And he said, 'There has to be suffering so that we will know joy.'

And I was like, 'Whoa!' That was so profound to say that in the middle of all that grief and loss.

"I think I agree with your statement. The reason we're in this life is to experience the separation, experience the disconnection, so that we will know connection. We will know true unity and joy," James says.

"I feel that so much," I say, realizing that choosing James as a subject to interview had led me down a beautiful but very deep path.

"I think your meeting with Sky that day was probably one of the most important, magical moments for her coming to Florida," I tell James. "She had moved here from California and had kind of a California mentality and was a little bitter about coming here, I think just because politics are different and she felt a little alienated and didn't know where she fit in. She was not Christian. She was almost resistant to that stuff, and yet we sat with you and you prayed with her. And it was like all of our differences just melted. You know? Any of her resistance just melted. We both felt that. I was really honored that we got—that *she* got—to feel that. So yeah, there's many levels of what I call magic, here. You can call it a lot of different things, but it's here. It's here."

"Thank you for that," James answers. "It was an honor for me to meet with her and to be able to relate to her because I had suffered through my son fighting cancer. So we were able to relate through suffering and find connection in the paradox of that, right?"

James continues, "To answer your question about what we want people to experience here, I'll use your word: we want people to feel known and *connected*. I hope that people will feel peace.

"I practice gratitude," he says. "I heard a quote, maybe six years ago, 'You can't see with spiritual eyes except through the lens of gratitude.'

"So, that's my question every day, and we talk about it as a staff before we even open. We all ask each other what we're grateful for today. It's like putting on a pair of glasses that give you a different perspective. When you put on gratefulness, you see differently. So, I hope people leave feeling grateful. And the setting helps too. I mean, the beauty of nature helps."

We both laugh, finding release in the moment after touching on some pretty heavy subjects. James then tells me about his former business in Wenshan, China, prior to 2018.

"We had a four-layer building. The bottom floor was a milk-tea shop with boba tea. And the second floor was a music shop, and the third floor was my floor. There was a recording studio. In the basement, there was a venue where we taught drum lessons and we'd do open-mic nights." I

"Oh my goodness," I say.

"It was a dream. It was like, yeah, firing on all cylinders of who I am, living on the edge of myself. You know, learning Chinese, singing Chinese songs in bars, and then recording Chinese artists and getting to produce their songs…and just being with that local group that became family.

"And then, in a turn of events, we were going to have our second child, and it was through spiritual dreams that I knew it was time to move home. And yeah, I was very resistant to that. I bawled for two days when I made the decision—which was somehow confirmation that was the right thing." He laughs.

"And in hindsight, it's like, 'Oh my gosh, we got rescued from having to live through COVID in China.' But [at the time], I didn't know the reason I was moving back.

"So yeah, I didn't have a job. We were planning on staying with my parents in Central Florida, but then my dad told us we were all moving to The Hammock instead, and suddenly we're in a new city.

"I tried many things. I interviewed for things. My wife works remotely, so she kind of supported us throughout it. I was a stay-at-home dad.

"That was an intense year. For a year, it was eleven of us, four generations in one house, just to make it work. It was a wilderness season for me because I had so much purpose with all that cool stuff I was telling you about in China. That was my identity!

"I wanted to provide for my family, and then all of a sudden, I'm living in my parents' house with my entire family, in one room with two kids…*and* one kid is a newborn!"

In 2019, James, as a musician, started finding gigs in St. Augustine. He soon had shows booked four or five nights a week and once again felt he had a purpose.

"But then 2020 hits, and the first thing to close were the bars where all of my work was. [I had] six months of gigs booked, and all of a sudden, they just got wiped away, along with all that income."

To make ends meet, James ended up selling all of his music equipment and once again faced losing another dream and along with it, another identity.

"So, it sent me on a journey of finding who I am, my identity outside of what I do. And I'm convinced that"—he pauses—"you know, I don't want to be thankful [for people's pain], but I have to be thankful when people go through trials or hit rock bottom because I believe sometimes the only catalyst for change is to suffer."

As James talks, I'm right there with him with every word. I can relate closely to what he says.

"I believe in resurrection," James says. "When there's death, there is resurrection. Out of 2020 and 2021, we started this business. I was struggling to find who I am, but my dad had a vision to do this. I said, 'I will come in and serve. And I will just learn the whole business.'

"I woke up every morning at five just to learn the business and start cooking. I learned from another chef, and a year later, that chef was gone and the keys were in my hand. And I'm like, 'Okay! I came here just to serve and to find out who I am, and now I'm running the whole thing.'"

He pauses and then says, "But my identity now is *not* a chef…it's *not* a musician…"

I lean forward, curious. "What is it?" I ask. "What is your identity? Have you figured it out?"

"You know, if I could put it into words just as I'm talking, it's 'friend.' Because every morning, I wake up and get to work with my friends. My mission is to wake up and be with my friends, to ask them what they're grateful for, and to work harder than them so that I can serve them well. So yeah, my identity is 'friend.' Through that lens, it doesn't matter what's thrown at me. If the business closes tomorrow, my purpose is still the same. I got to do this with my friends."

James then returns to the resurrection story he had started earlier.

"So I had mentioned I had to sell all of my music equipment to make ends meet during that time. It was devastating. But on our one-year birthday of the café, I got a couple pieces of plywood and some pallets, and I built a stage and booked one of my musician friends. We had live music on our café's one-year birthday, which was a resurrection because what had died all of a sudden became resurrected. And I got to jam out that day. And then, fast forward, we wanted more music, so we built a bigger stage. And now, me and my friends get to play live music every Sunday.

"I found in a journal from like ten years ago, one of my dreams was to own a live-music venue. And I was like, 'Oh my gosh, it had to die before resurrection.' And I realized all the music equipment that I've gotten to purchase since opening the café is double what I had to sell.

"I was like, 'Oh my gosh, this is *more* than a resurrection!' But what I had to lose, and the pain and depression that I had to go through of losing that identity, all had to happen for this pure thing to happen.

"Now I don't have to go out and look for gigs. I get to play, and I get to invite my friends in. It looks a little different. I start smoking meat at five a.m. so that I can play music by nine on a Sunday. It's not what I thought my dreams were, but I'm living my dream."

Ragga Surf Café
9700 N Ocean Shore Blvd
Marineland, FL 32060
(904) 274-1962
www.raggasurfcafe.com

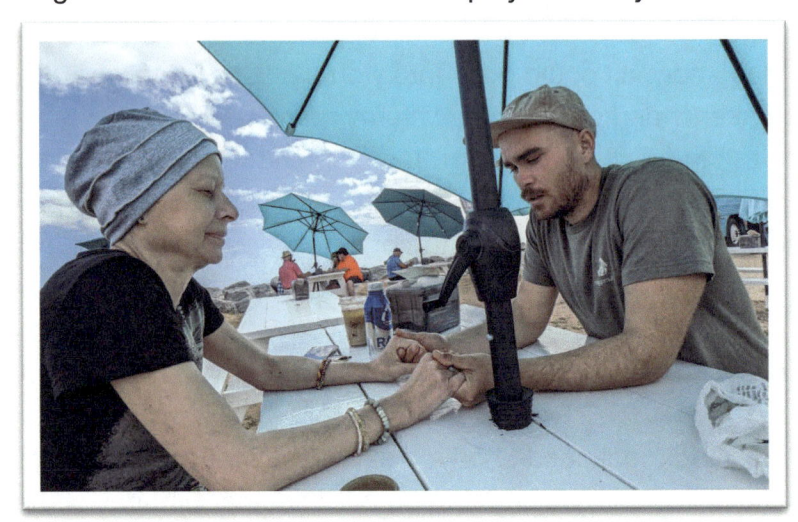

Denise Hagan
Raining Wildflowers, LLC
The Hammock, Florida

Tonic for a Broken Heart

After talking with James, I drive south along A1A towards Sea Colony, a gated community in The Hammock, just a few miles from Ragga. I drive down a long road surrounded by oaks and palms and pull up to a guard station. I show the man my ID, and the gate lifts. Along the road, the dense line of trees recedes, and I find myself driving through an open and pristine, purposely laid-out neighborhood where well-planned parks, canals, and ponds delineate sections of the community.

I follow Denise's directions, looking for "the house without a lawn" as she described in her text. As I drive, I note that all of the other houses have neatly kept lawns except one. It is, instead, planted with dense and wild ground cover. The low-lying plants that make up the small yard are dotted by tiny exotic purple flowers. When it occurs to me that this unique home is, in fact, Denise's, I smile. Although I have not yet met Denise, I realize that she's got to be a bit of a rebel to have this sort of lawn in a gated community.

I knock on the door, and a kind-looking woman with long, straight, silvery hair, neatly trimmed bangs, and bright, shining eyes comes to the door. She welcomes me with a smile.

About a week ago, Denise had seen my post on Facebook sharing that I was looking for people to interview. She messaged me, telling me she lived near A1A and had a business called Raining Wildflowers. This is all I know about her.

"Hi, Becky," she says in her gentle voice as she opens the door. "Come on in."

After offering me some tea, she guides me into her kitchen to a small two-person table. We sit down and begin our conversation.

"So, tell me about your business," I say

"When my husband was dying…" She pauses as if holding back tears, and I realize her husband's death must still feel a little fresh and raw. I wait for her to continue. "He was always my biggest fan. He told me, 'You need to do something other than just working all the time. You need to explore your other interests.' I had been working for forty-three years in the financial industry. I had a practice. Typically I helped women who made financial decisions but were concerned about making a wrong one. I did stocks and bonds and insurance and all that stuff, but the planning was the important part. I did that all the time…and it was wonderful. A lot of my clients became my friends.

"But, getting back to my husband, he passed away two years ago last week, June 11th. And so I took what he said to heart. I was surfing Facebook one day in early September and an ad came up from Rosemary Gladstar. She's kind of considered the fairy godmother of herbalism in America. I've always been a huge fan, even before the internet, because I loved gardening.

"My husband used to help me with my gardening. He would be my labor. He would say, 'I'm your mule. So whatever you need done, I'll do.' He constructed all these beautiful gardens, and I'd just plop the plants in, and it was beautiful. I had this gorgeous herb garden laid out with bricks in a cute little pattern right outside my kitchen in the Midwest.

"Since I have this practical bent and most of my decisions are based on my stomach, my first [question] was to ask, 'How can I use these in a culinary way? How can I eat this stuff?'

"You know, you read stuff [about the healing properties of herbs], and you're like, 'Yeah, yeah, yeah. Is that really true?' But then you start seeing something happen." She continues, "There was this plant called comfrey, which is gorgeous. The hummingbirds loved it. It's just like a beautiful plant with beautiful purple blooms. In the Midwest, you couldn't kill it. It would just grow all over the place.

"It was supposed to be used for wound healing and even for healing broken bones and stuff like that. And again you're like, 'Yeah, right,'" she says with a cynical tone.

"So I'm racing to get some gardening done, and I scratched myself with a wire. I was wearing shorts, and I scratched my thigh with a pretty big scratch—you know, kind of like a deep cat scratch. And those things, they take forever to heal, but I didn't have time to get it cleaned out. So I just spit on it and I grabbed a leaf of one of these plants and I rubbed it over my leg. It was kind of scratchy. It didn't sting, but it was scratchy like little barbs. And then I went about my day.

"Well, the next day, the scratch completely disappeared! I was like, 'Whoa, this works!'

"My husband tore his Achilles tendon halfway and healed it without surgery. It took a while; it wasn't like an instantaneous thing. [But] before he died, he was back to running three 5- or 10Ks a week."

She continues, "So he dies, and I see this ad for this program on the science and art of herbalism." Denise points to a document on her kitchen counter and tells me, "I actually have the certificate up there, if you want to look at it."

Denise then says, "So I threw myself into this program, and I was still doing my financial practice."

"And are you in grief at the same time?" I ask.

"Oh, yes, absolutely. Absolutely," she says. "So one of the subject areas was on nervous-system health. [The nervous system] affects mood as well as physical issues. I was definitely in a funk. I'm not talking about, like, 'Oh, I feel a little sad.' There would be days in a row, like three days in a row, where I was knocked down, dragged out, crying.

"I have a very emotional friend, and when she's happy or she's sad, she's always blubbering. She's one of those people, and I love her, but I remember calling her once and saying, 'I'm going to challenge you to a snot fest.'

"I know it's a normal process to go through grief, and I wasn't trying to self-medicate it or anything like that. I actually wanted to feel it. I didn't want to stuff it down. I wanted it to get out. But I got to thinking, 'You know, there's got to be something that can help me.' Also, in conjunction with that [in our coursework], you had to demonstrate proficiency in order to get through the course. So you had to create formulas for teas because teas are the easiest ways to get herbs into your system.

"So I really intently researched this whole thing. And because I'm driven by my stomach, I said 'This cannot taste like medicine. It has to taste good. It has to taste nice.' I didn't want something that would make you loopy and be hallucinogenic or make it so you couldn't operate machinery. I just wanted a food that would help me with this. And so I made this blend I called Joyful Tea. It has wonderful herbs that are uplifting for your mood without making you unable to focus. And it tastes good.

"One of [the ingredients] is really good for your heart. Not just emotionally, but physically. And another one is really good for a broken heart or achiness. It's uplifting. Another one is designed for not just anxious nerves, but for completely frayed, frazzled nerves. It's *really* good for that."

Denise then clarifies, "This is not me saying this; these are herbalists with hundreds of years of experience. I do have to say, I'm not a medical doctor. I do not practice medicine. This is educational only. Because it's illegal to practice herbalism in the United States. I just love plants. Let's just say that.

"So anyway, I'm just doing this for myself, and what I found with the Joyful Tea is that it didn't make me feel bubbly. It leveled out the lows, and I did feel better. I would still have moments in a day where I'd see something that brings up a memory, and I'd just have to go through that, but I did feel better with it.

"I had a friend who was having a garden party, and she said, 'I want you to serve herbal teas.'" Denise explains that she agreed to share her teas at the party. Joyful Tea became a huge hit. "I had one of the people say to me, 'If you ever make this to sell, I will buy it.'"

Denise eventually completed herbalism school and began her business called Raining Wildflowers, selling teas along with organic creams and all-natural insect repellent.

I then ask Denise to talk more about the grieving process.

"When you lose somebody that you're so close to for all those years…um…I knew, intellectually, there would be challenges, but I had no idea emotionally how impactful it would be. And I don't know, maybe other people are better at foreseeing what that would be like before it happens. But I wasn't. I just got hit with a brick wall.

"Part of what I was trying to figure out was my purpose, because I was expecting that for at least another fifteen years, you know, we'd be together because he was so healthy.

"I was like, 'Okay, what am I supposed to do?' I read so many books. I did so much research into how to find your purpose. I was really struggling, like, 'What the heck am I supposed to be doing?' I would pray about it."

It wasn't until Denise discovered a prayer card in a book that a friend had given her that she found just what she needed.

"When I read (the prayer) a year after Ed died, I was like, 'Are you kidding me? This prayer has been here all the time?' You know, it's sort of like how they say something appears to you when you're ready to receive it. I guess I wasn't ready to receive it that first year."

She pulls out the prayer and reads it to me:

"O, Holy Spirit. Beloved of my soul. I adore you. Enlighten me. Guide me. Protect me. Console me. Tell me what I should do. Give me your orders and I promise to submit myself entirely to you. Let me only know your will."

After reading, she explains, "What I realized is that I *didn't* need to be looking for the thing that would dictate the course of the rest of my life."

As we talked, she stood up and went to her fridge and read a small note she had written for herself after Ed's death. In place of finding a single purpose, she would follow this philosophy. She read it out loud: "Pretend everything you do is *the* most important task of your life."

She explains, "So if I'm mopping the floor, that is the most important thing in my life, and that helps me focus on what I'm doing instead of fretting about what I'm supposed to be doing. Instead of just going through the motions during the day, I actually do stuff. So if I'm creating this tea, if I'm blending it, I'm concentrating on exactly getting the right blend of the various plants in it."

"The first time I drove up to my office after Ed died, it was the weirdest feeling because I was looking around and was like, 'This is the first time I'm driving up North A1A as a widow.'"

Denise pauses then begins again with slow and deep reflection, "It was the weirdest surrealistic feeling. When I was driving up to work, I thought, 'Okay, I'm in a play…we're all in a play'—you know, the Shakespeare thing, 'All the world's a stage.' I have to play my part, remaining in the play until I die or, using the play analogy, until they kill my character off. If I'm here, playing this part, what is my part supposed to be? What do I put into my performance?

"Sometimes I get clearer on that notion than others. But when I'm experiencing something [with another person], I ask myself, 'How can they benefit from having encountered me? What am I supposed to learn from this to be a better person than I was the day before?' Because, otherwise, I feel that existence is a complete waste of time and effort and resources. It's like, why would my soul have decided to come into this body at this time? Because obviously, there was some work that needed to be done."

After our conversation, Denise and I walk out to her garden. I'm impressed by how peaceful and bright she appears when she stands beside her herbs. I take a few photos. Before leaving, Denise gives me a sample of the Joyful Tea, and I head home.

Raining Wildflowers, LLC

www.Rainingwildflowers.com

June 20th, 2024

Becky's Journal

Something Magnificent

I'm at home now. The last three interviews I've conducted appear to be more than just the quick little stories about the area I had initially anticipated. Instead, something deeper, more intimate, more authentic is emerging. It seems the stories themselves are pulling me in a deeper direction.

It appears that any time I hand my life over to the Universe…God…The Great Spirit (insert your preferred term here), something magnificent yet oddly out of my control begins to happen. Everything I need comes at me…and fast.

Since my divorce, authentic connection and intimacy have been things I've craved, and to my surprise, here it is! But rather than arriving in the form of one single person, what I yearned for has arrived in the form of all these beautiful people, guests who have kindly volunteered to share their stories and perspectives.

But something else is happening too. As much as I had hoped to avoid my own inner struggles and instead just plummet head-first into the stories of others, the opposite is happening.

Being with people who are so open and vulnerable is, for better or worse, cracking me open in ways I never anticipated. It seems the more I listen, the more I realize I'm not alone. Our stories and backgrounds may be completely different, and yet it's through our humanity, our deep and rich-lived experience, that we can open up and truly connect.

I'm not sure where this book is headed, but it seems the more I stay open to the possibilities, the deeper, the greater…the richer the reward.

It's starting to seem that my little book about A1A is gifting me with more riches than I ever could have imagined.

June 22, 2024

Voice Memo to a Friend

Hey, Derrick!

I'm completely baffled by this book project. It's writing itself. This morning, while I was getting my coffee at Debra Jean's, the owner, Jeremie, came by and started telling me her life philosophy. I had assumed because of her religious background that her views would not resonate, but it looks like she's discovered truths about life similar to my own but via a very different route.

People just start talking to me now before I have my recorder set up. I can't possibly capture it all! I realize the time is really ripe for a book like this. With our elections coming up in November, it sometimes feels to me like there's some external force in the world that "wants" to keep us angry and divided. If I can write a book that does the opposite—and simply celebrates connection and the beauty of the human spirit—I've done a good thing.

PART III

"Listen to the music of the moment,
people dance and sing
We're just one big family
And it's our God-forsaken right to be loved, loved, loved, loved, loved"

–Lyrics from "I'm Yours"
by Jason Mraz

AyoLane Halusky

Earth Kinship Kayak Tours & Nature Education
The Matanzas Inlet, Florida

Kinship Redefined

I arrive at the Inlet Beach and General Store this morning not for work, but instead for my next interview. Janine had given me the thumbs up to use the back room to meet with AyoLane, a kayaking and nature guide in the area.

When I arrive at the shop, Adam is behind the counter in a Hawaiian shirt and flip-flops. He is turned towards the back wall, watching his phone, which is precariously propped up on the coffee maker. At first, I think he is watching a video until he starts talking. He isn't speaking in his playful Adam-the-Pun-Making-Boat-Captain voice that I'm used to. Instead, he is focused and deliberate.

"I make a motion: all those in favor, say 'Aye.'"

I later learn that Adam sits on the executive committee for the Florida Wildlife Federation, chairing their policy committee. He is apparently leading an important Zoom meeting. His sister-in-law, Renne, the store manager, usually works Tuesdays but is out of town, so Adam is doing double duty, leading a meeting *and* helping customers in the shop.

A few minutes after my arrival, the front door chimes and AyoLane enters the shop, wearing his telltale Panama-style hat with a white egret feather tucked in its brim, his long, blonde hair hanging down his back. Even in a t-shirt and shorts, he appears less like a modern ecotour guide and more like a French explorer or a medicine man who has just arrived via time machine from the sixteenth century. I notice two intricate snake tattoos curling around his forearms.

I know AyoLane (pronounced io-lan-ay) only from Facebook. His photos of the backwater kayak trips he leads with his business, Earth Kinship Kayak Tours and Nature Education, have always enticed me. I was thrilled to learn that he hosts trips not only to the north of us in St. Johns County but also near me, along the Matanzas River that runs parallel to A1A.

I know AyoLane is a great storyteller, connected to the Native Americans who have inhabited this area since long before European settlers came. But aside from these small notions, I know little else.

"So tell me a little bit about you," I say as we situate ourselves on two folding chairs in the back room, surrounded by a backstock of sunscreen, travel mugs, and kids' lifejackets.

"I grew up in what was previously called Fruit Cove, when it was still old houses," AyoLane says. "There was no such thing as an HOA at that time." He smirks and adds, "Thank God."

"The closest grocery store was twenty miles away. That whole area was pretty much just old homes and wilderness and a two-lane road. We had a veterinarian and a couple small shops and little produce places along the way, but there wasn't much out there."

"So you're talking, like, thirty years ago?" I ask.

"This is in the '70s and '80s. I was born in '74. I was actually born in Crawfordville, which is in Tallahassee. We came here when I was one or so years old. So I didn't know anything different than Fruit Cove.

"My father [Joe Halusky] was an IFAS Extension Sea Grant Agent—a marine biologist who worked with Whitney Labs in Marineland at the Marine Education Center.

"There used to be this big bubble building [in Marineland]. I think they now park RVs there. It was one of those buildings built to withstand a hurricane. That was my father's office."

"Did you ever get to go to work with your dad?"

"Oh yeah. I kind of grew up there. I would be there all the time. It's the first place I saw a sunrise, down by the rocks [on the beach], where all the coquina rocks come out," he says

"So tell me about your connection with the land," I say with a bit of hesitancy. "I realize this might be a big question."

"Um, yeah…how do you start that?" he says, thinking. "Um, I've always been interested in nature. As children, as we look at our society and our culture and as we're growing up, there's a lot of questions. There's a lot of concerns. There's a lot of seeing the dangers. So often [when we're little kids] and hear the stories, what are we most interested in? The monster of the story. What's most attractive is usually not the protagonist; it could be the villain."

AyoLane goes on to explain how important it was for him as a child to understand the role of the villain. He felt it helped him better understand the dangerous, threatening things in life.

"Fruit Cove in Northeast Florida was very controlled by the churches and the religious orders. There were so many different orders. And they were very, very [focused on] what's right and wrong.

"I think when I was about eight years old, I finally understood what they were saying sin was. I had been called a sinner. My mom wanted me to grow up in the church ever since I was really little. As a child, I just didn't understand it. I just bypassed it in my mind. But when I was about eight, that's when I really became angry. Because I was like, 'Wait a minute, I don't lie. I don't cheat. I don't steal at all. I don't do all these things you say I do. Why are you pointing your finger at me?' Like, 'Wait, what's going on here?'

"So I started to really question these authoritarian religions telling me who I am. I didn't agree with it.

"I had a grandfather who was very interested in hunting and being out in nature. Sometimes he wouldn't even carry his rifle going out there. Sometimes [he would go] just to get out there. And he hunted arrowheads…in Pennsylvania, by the way. So I would go visit him, and he would come and visit me. That's when I started to understand there's different ways to look at this world. You know, it's not one book telling us what's right and wrong.

"There is [instead] what works and what doesn't work. Obviously, if we're doing illegal activities, it doesn't work in our society, but we've got to look at things in a different perspective, so my perspective was broadened at an early age."

AyoLane explains it was at this point he began to question when it was safe for him to share his perspectives, which he could see weren't following the mainstream views of the people around him.

"So nature became my church. Nature became my spirituality. Nature became my connection. We had six acres of wilderness that were behind all the houses in a loop on Lakewood Drive in Fruit Cove, and that became my area for exploring nature.

"There was Cunningham Creek. There was Julington Creek. There were all these swamps in the area and wilderness areas that I would explore, too, when I got older. But having that in my back yard, I literally could just walk out into the woods, and that's where I would spend most of my time.

"I can remember in grade school, one of the first questions I was asked was a separating question: Are you a Gator or are you a Dog? And I was so confused because my family didn't watch football. We didn't get involved with sports like that. It just never was an interest. I had intellectuals for parents. They were academics.

"My mom was a 4-H agent for Duval County. My dad was a marine biologist. So we talked about different things. We didn't talk about who won the game last week.

"Georgia Bulldogs or Florida Gators? That was *the* thing. Like, if you're not one or the other, then you're ostracized. If you're a Dog and you're with Gator people, then you are an enemy.

"This is in grade school. These kids didn't even really know what football was, but their parents were so hardcore about it. That's how the kids started identifying each other, and that's when I first started learning about social groups and being in or being out of certain social groups.

"I was one of those people that played on the fringes. I would jump around between all the different groups. *Revenge of the Nerds* came out, and suddenly nerds became cool. It was a weird time in society.

"When I realized there were no groups who were talking about my view of spirituality, I started to shift and started going in negative ways. You know, smoking pot, drinking. I mean, at an early age. I was smoking cigarettes at twelve.

"Why did I do that? To numb out. I had to numb the spirituality because it was so powerful in my world that I couldn't really talk about it. So I had to numb it for a few years."

"So you said you were numbing out the spirituality. What do you mean by that?" I ask.

He pauses to reflect and then speaks slowly. "When I walked into the woods, it was almost like communication on a different level. Nowadays, we can understand it because there's a lot of people that are interested in energetics.

"At that time? No way. You're a witch. You were burned at the stake. You were ostracized. I mean, the church groups were brutal. So you had to be really careful about what you said and who you said it to. And so you just shut up. They called it 'pretend,' even though I felt like trees could communicate with me. There was definitely a connection. I would climb them and feel them, you know? Animals would come right up to me. You just didn't do this where other people would see you.

"My dad was a big influence on me because he was also a philosopher on the side. We had a library in our house, and there was everything from Taoist and Buddhist teachings to the Quran. Every [country] that we went to war with, he got their religious text and would read it. So every religious and every philosophy text was in the house. I had access to lots of different things—Native American included.

"One time, my father and his best friend, who was a poet, got together. So you had a scientist and an artist drinking a bottle of rum, and they came up with an idea to create a conference. This conference was going to bring arts and science together to talk about healing the Earth.

"So they were like, 'Okay, we're seeing the signs. Let's talk about it. Let's get together and talk about [caring for the Earth].' So they created the Earth Stewardship Conference. It was a one-or two-day conference where they would just get minds together and they'd have a keynote speaker. Around the second year, religions started becoming involved. So, it was art, science, and religions…or spiritualities."

"What year was this?" I ask.

"Eighty-eight or eighty-nine. My dad used to go talk to religious orders as a marine biologist and say, 'You know you're destroying our river. You have these big beautiful churches, and you have this ground that you mow, and you put chemicals and fertilizers on them, and you have this huge parking lot. Doesn't your book talk about going to nature? Isn't that where the kingdom of God is?' At that time, that was a cutting-edge thing to say. And some of them started listening.

"A nun actually was on the steering committee, and she said, 'The name [Earth Stewardship] is incorrect.' My dad asked the nun her suggestion for a name, and she said, 'Let's think about what the word *stewardship* really means. A steward over an industry knows how machines work. They can fine-tune them to get them to work the most efficiently. A steward knows their shop. But we have no idea what happens on this earth. We're just starting to learn how this earth actually works, and we call ourselves stewards?'

"'No, I guess we really can't,' they all agreed. We're just children in a sandbox, fighting over toys and not really agreeing that we're in a sandbox and we're all equal. That's the problem. And so, the Earth Stewardship Conference realized that we're not here to heal the Earth. *We're here to heal the humans.*

"When the humans can come from a healing spot—forgiveness and compassion—*then* we can actually work towards stewardship at some point...maybe thousands of years in the future. But we're not there. No way we can be there.

"So instead of *stewardship,* the organization came up with the word *kinship*.

"If you think about the word *kin*, it could mean love, it could mean understanding. But it usually means family. 'I *kin* you' is an old Appalachian saying, meaning I understand what you're saying...or I love you. It also means that I've taken you on as my family.

"'*Ko-la*' in Lakota languages means friend, but it's beyond blood. We're connecting at a higher level. Or '*mitauye oyasin,*' which is a Lakota term for extended family, means we might not be blood, we weren't born in the same blood, but we agree on our views and we've taken each other on. It's where I'm willing to be there for your mistakes and you're willing to be there for mine. And I'm going to help bring you up to a higher level and you're going to help me. So, we're holding each other in integrity. There's a commitment that's happening. It's not just a bypass.

"So kinship is a respect. It also allows you to make mistakes. If you keep making mistakes over and over, that's not a mistake; that's a habit. But if you can make a mistake and go, 'Oh, I recognize that I need to change,' that's kinship. So if we could be in kinship with the world and each other, yeah, then maybe we can actually move somewhere."

AyoLane continues, "So that conference ran for about sixteen years. It was before its time."

"Where were those meetings held?" I ask.

"At a bunch of different places in Northeast Florida [including Marineland]. It brought in people from Australia, people from Africa. Native American elders started to come.

Scientists started to come. It was a lot of people who were talking about the Earth and talking about community, and talking about not trashing our backyards…and not trashing ourselves. It was coming to recognize that we need to heal ourselves.

"It wasn't psychotherapy, you know, but it was scientific based. It was also arts based and was religious or spiritual based. So it had kind of this cool mixture."

"So, will you tell me more about your Native American connection and your personal connection with the Earth?" I ask.

AyoLane thinks for a moment.

"Any core issue that any of us are born with or raised with is our greatest gift to the world when we can go through it and we can see the gift that we were given.

"Sometimes [the core gifts] are harder to see than others. I mean, situations are very individual and can be very brutal at times. So we can't compare our situation to another person's situation. We can just have our experience.

"Through the Earth Kinship Conference, I met some Native elders, whom I became family with. One specific gentleman—his name is Chobie—I met while another elder was telling a story. When we met each other, he looked at me goes, 'I know you,' and I was like, 'I know you too.' And he goes, 'Let's go for a walk.' And we were like brothers. I was fifteen [or] sixteen, and he was in his thirties. But it was like, *I knew this man*, like…I don't know…I couldn't explain it. It's like meeting somebody I already knew. We both recognized it.

"So I used to go down and spend time with his wife and his two kids. I was kind of like an uncle to them for a long time. I got invited to green corn ceremonies, and hunter ceremonies, and things like that. I started to learn the songs, and I started to learn how they connected to the seasons and then learned their old stories.

"These were Muscogees, who are originally from the Georgia/South Carolina/Alabama area. But when the Trail of Tears and all that stuff happened, and the Natives in Florida were demolished and killed or put into slavery, most of the people went to Oklahoma or went the other direction. Some of the Muscogees came down in here…

"These were some of the ones that had to hide in the swamps and integrated in different ways. So a lot of their major, large ceremonies had disappeared. A lot of their knowledge of it had disappeared. There were certain secret ceremonies that they kept, that were still around."

AyoLane then asks me, "Did you know that Natives were not allowed to practice their own tradition until *1978*?"

"What?!" I ask, surprised. "In Florida or in the United States?"

"In the United States—1978. You could be hung, killed, or put in prison until 1978, when it became 'legal' to be Native, to practice your tradition.

"The United States was based on a lot of genocide. Genocide is our foundation, unfortunately, but we can change that attitude if we want.

"So you asked me about my connection to Native People and to the Earth. I'm telling you all of this stuff because as a child…as a young adult…as a teenager, *these* are the stories that I'm hearing about Florida. *These* are the connections that I'm hearing."

"So were you hearing the Native American history?" I ask.

"I'm not hearing someone say 'Oh, in 19—, such and such happened' or 'so and so went here.' No, I'm hearing *the pain,* and I'm seeing the reaction in *real* time.

"I call these 'ripples of genocide.' I watched it as an outsider. You know, I'm white. I'm about as white as…I've got seven bloods of white in me, you know, but I've I watched this," AyoLane says intently. "I was one of those quiet kids that would just listen and pay attention. The elders were always willing to talk if you were willing to listen.

"I remember talking to this man, one time. He claimed to be a hundred and five. His sister was older than him. I remember sitting with him, asking at age sixteen or seventeen, 'Are you concerned about your stories and your traditions disappearing?' Because that's what we were seeing.

"And he looked at me long and hard and kind of leaned back against this tree and wiped the sweat off his brow. He smiled and said, 'Where do you think we heard it from? Where do you think we got these from?' He says, 'Do *you* have the ability to walk out into the woods and listen? Can you hear the wind singing? Can you hear the whispers in the woods? Can you *feel* the energy of the springs? That's where we got these from. It's out there if you're willing to listen. Our [stories] and traditions might come and go, but they are still out there. It's the hard way to learn because you have to go through it to really understand it and learn, but they're not going to die, because they're out there.'"

AyoLane continues, "The confidence that he had that the spirit that moves through the wilderness can't be killed, can't be crushed, was nice. It was nice and refreshing to feel this from a hundred-and-something-year-old person. I mean, that was comforting to me as a kid, and I was really about sustaining these old teachings and sustaining these connections to the natural world.

"So I spent a lot of time with the Muscogees. There was another man in Jacksonville. He used to pour *inipis*, Lakota sweat lodges. He was Muskogee, white, *and* Lakota, which is kind of interesting. I spent a lot of time in the sweat lodge ceremonies in Jacksonville. It probably was what saved my life.

"Going back to that time of numbing myself out: when I came into the Earth Kinship Conference, when my dad was running it and I met these elders, I started hearing the things that I used to think about when I was five and six years old…eight years old, when I was running around the woods. And I'm like, 'Wait a minute. I was called crazy for thinking these things—that trees communicate and that animals have consciousness. And here's these Native elders talking about communication with trees and communication with the natural world and this energy flow that moves through everything, *including us*!'

"I was like, 'Okay, I'm not crazy. I can come out of this self-induced numbing and come back into accepting this perception that was given to me as a little kid.

"It never left, even during the numbing, but here I was freer and allowed to experience it because I had seventy-, eighty-, one-hundred-year-old people around me that were living it, or trying to live it.

"And so, that shifted a lot of things for me. I was not a self-induced prisoner in myself or a prisoner from societal expectations, a prisoner of the Southern belles, and the church-related groups that were in the area.

"I remember during that eight-year-old time, I asked my dad, 'Can I not go to church anymore?' And he said, 'Well, you have a choice—quiet time at home, or you can go visit other churches with your friends.' So I did *that*. I went to every church that I could go to with all my friends, and they all said the same thing. They talked more about the devil and evil than they did about good and love. I just was like, 'Why are you all so attracted to evil? Like, I don't understand why y'all speak so much about it.' Now we know that the more we speak about something, the more reality it becomes. Like that should have been a teaching back then. I was like, 'I can't do this.'

"But in nature, I didn't see any evil out there, you know? Of course, a panther kills something to eat, but that's not evil. There's this communication. There's this understanding between predator and prey."

At this point in the conversation with AyoLane, I'm completely awestruck. AyoLane comes from a radically different life experience than myself; however, he speaks about many things I have felt deeply but never spoken about.

"You've heard of Joseph Campbell?" he asks, and my heart brightens.

"Of course," I say. Joseph Campbell has been my favorite teacher since I was in college.

AyoLane states, "Joseph Campbell was the leading PhD in the power of mythology in America. He did a six-hour interview [for PBS] two weeks before he died. I listened to that quite often because I believe he was a true elder."

AyoLane recounts the video.

"'We need a new mythology,' Campbell said. 'We have the Adam and Eve mythology. We have thousands of mythologies from all over.'"

The 1988 interview series that AyoLane refers to is titled The Power of Myth. In it, journalist Bill Moyers had asked Campbell when he thought the new myth will arise.

AyoLane recounts Campbell's answer: "Well, the world is moving too fast right now. We're colliding cultures. We're running into each other. Religions are having difficulties. Until that destruction happens and it settles back down and we can become a *world* unit—not France versus Germany versus Irish versus…whatever, you know? When we can stop separating ourselves and become a world unit, a world consciousness, then we can maybe slow down enough to have a new mythology, and that new mythology will carry us on."

AyoLane continues, "He's just talking about an awakening. But what would cause that? It would have to be an external force. I think humans are intelligent enough to come to the conclusion without needing some [destructive] external force forcing us together…but we're just not ready yet.

"We're still working towards this direction. And it's a lot of suffering. We're just going to have to work through it together until we're ready. I don't think one religion is going to do it. I don't think one scientific fact is going to do it. And I'm damn sure it ain't going to be a politician that's going to do it."

For another half an hour or so, AyoLane and I hung out in the back room at the Inlet Store, discussing these big concepts that I have devoted a great deal of time in my life to reflecting on.

After driving home, inspired by our conversation, I pull out my personal notes on Joseph Campbell. Less than a month earlier, I had watched the exact clip from The Power of Myth that AyoLane referred to. Deeply inspired by it back then, I had written these notes:

> There is a new mythology rising. It is one of self that is connected to all.
> We are on a human journey that is connected to a greater path beyond our comprehension. This myth is a collective story hidden in each of our hearts.
> It is through each other that this myth can be born, and yet, it's already here. As individuals listen to their hearts, we are learning its song. By sharing and talking

and connecting, we can express it. It is beyond words. However, it is through our connection on the human plane that awakens it within.

It occurs to me, after rereading my notes, that my desire to talk with others in deep and meaningful ways exists because I really do believe our collective truth, the *new mythology* we all crave, exists within each of our hearts. Every time we connect with a fellow human, a piece of that story is revealed, less with words and more with energy.

Just as the hundred-and-five-year-old elder explained to AyoLane when he was a kid, the stories are out there, whispering to us—yes, in the wind, yes, through the rushing waters, but also through each other.

This is why I exist. This is my mission: to listen and share the secret spoken and unspoken stories we all have to share.

> The myth has been emerging; it's been asking to be born. We can piece it together through each other. We are the vehicle for this myth. And maybe, just maybe, it is through our collective story that we as a people can heal.

Earth Kinship Kayak Tours & Nature Education
5880 Don Manuel Rd
Elkton, FL 32033
(904) 477-5669
www.earthkinship.us

June 26th, 2024

Becky's Journal

The New Myth Rising

I'm at home, and my house is very quiet. I've been sitting in my favorite pink and orange paisley chair, overlooking the river, writing from my phone for over an hour. The sun has set, and it's now dark outside.

I'm rereading my notes and seeing so many patterns in these stories. Somehow, I have inadvertently discovered a series of people who have used their personal struggles to propel themselves out beyond their own difficulties into a space of healing for themselves and others.

These people have suffered, lost themselves, and then found themselves through the power of connection. And they have now been able to share their gifts with the community at large.

The funny thing is, my house is quiet and I am alone, but I don't feel lonely. In fact, I feel more deeply connected than I ever thought possible. What a puzzling thing to be alone but feel so full, so deeply connected.

Maybe Melinda's statement about me needing a job was less about a need for employment and more about a purpose. The purpose I've been searching for most of my life seems to have somehow inexplicably found me. It's weaving itself into these words as I write to you.

June 27th, 2024

Becky's Journal

A few hours after my last entry, I snuggled into bed. I had remembered that the Trump-Biden presidential debate was starting, so I opened my phone to YouTube and watched it. Seeing these two older men on the stage act like boys on a playground did not settle well. I think it affected me deeply, much more than I would think a political event like this should.

I tossed and turned last night and eventually fell asleep.

I woke up this morning and felt a deep, unnamable sorrow. I have always had trouble debating political issues with people because I can see different perspectives. Similarly, I have trouble refuting anyone's religious or spiritual beliefs. I feel belief systems and the realities we create around them are highly personal, formed from our unique upbringings and our environments.

As Joseph Campbell has talked about, we're all living by different stories, and yet, when you get down to it, there's a thread connecting the stories of the world; there's a thread between our human hearts that can't be divided.

I feel we are losing touch with that thread. We are getting lost in a system that is too big, too thick, too layered. We are becoming more detached from our roots, from our souls, and we are forgetting to see each other. As both AyoLane and Bob had recognized in their younger years, it's not about one team versus another…it's about all of us.

I'm embarrassed to say I spent the morning at home crying. Sometimes it's hard for me to parse out whether my sadness is something personal or something I feel for society at large.

Either way, not wanting to dwell any longer in it, I slipped some clothes on and headed out the door. I didn't know exactly where I was going, but I knew stewing alone at home any longer would be my downfall.

I found myself in my little Nissan Juke heading north on A1A towards the Matanzas Inlet. I remembered I had left some food in the fridge at work, so I decided to stop at The Inlet Store.

It was a slow day, and Adam was once again behind the counter. With few visitors that morning, we talked politics for a bit. It was interesting to hear Adam's take on the debates and the state of the world. His knowledge goes deep.

We talked for a while, and I noticed the heaviness I'd felt this morning had lifted. I never mentioned to Adam how troubled I had been earlier today. I didn't need to. I'm just grateful to have good people around.

June 30th, 2024

Voice Memo

Hello. Good afternoon! I am driving down A1A, recording this voice memo. I don't know what this book is going to be, really, but so far I'm liking it. Things feel freaking intense…I think that it's a good thing.

Since the presidential debate…I don't know…I think the more I'm with people, the more interviews I do, the more I realize, "Oh, we're good. This is all good." We just have to surround ourselves with the good. We have to look for people who are being positive. We have to look for people who are channeling the good parts of themselves.

We all have shadow. For sure, we all have shadow, but there's also this beautiful, bright, and shiny part of us. It's why I love this area so much. I feel like so many people are in that space of goodness. And maybe that's just my perception of it, but I see it when I sit with people. I can see their beauty, and I can see their healthiness. I see that spark. We all have it. It's just a question of whether we choose to nurture it, tend to it, and feed it. Like building a warm fire, we need to care for it and let it grow.

I find when I go into my personal space of sadness, I sometimes get overwhelmed by my feelings and I begin to doubt myself. I get angry at myself. In my dark times, I come to believe that I'm unlovable, that I'm all alone in this stuff, that no one out there experiences these terrible, dark, mysterious, unnamable feelings like I do. That's when things feel scary and isolating.

But we have this choice—a very exciting choice!

We have the choice to feed the isolation, to feed the shadow feelings. Or we can look at the shadow feelings and say, "Yes, there is shadow. Yes, there is hardship. Yes, there is loneliness. All of these things are real, and all of it's okay."

But every time we make a connection with each other, with another human, with nature, with our own bodies, with our world, we no longer feel quite so lost. That's what this is all about. That's what this book is about.

I'm hoping to remind us, through a silly little book, that we're all human. We're all doing this. We're all beautiful. We're all…we're all fucked up. But we also have the potential for so much good. So let's keep feeding the good, man.

Let's keep feeding the good.

Tovah Janovski
Hope in the Wilderness—Gospel Message Outreach
Flagler Beach, Florida

I Came Upon a Child of God

I arrive at Sip and Surf early, buy a coffee, and choose a table outside with a view of the ocean.

Tovah is a fellow writer I met over a decade ago through the Inspired Mic, a Flagler County-based open mic that provided a stage for writers to share their words and reflections. Through it, we built a strong writers' community.

At the time of the Inspired Mic, Tovah was in her early seventies. She would amble up on stage and, like a comedian, tell hilarious stories from her youth. Sometimes she would sing. Other times, she'd tell religious stories. Either way, we always knew it was going to be a good performance.

Tovah has devoted the past several years to sharing the Christian gospel every Thursday at the picnic tables along the beach near The Funky Pelican in Flagler Beach. It tickles me that I have a friend who is one of *those* people. For myself, growing up as a good Jewish girl, evangelical Christian folks always fascinated me, but I was reminded to keep my distance. And to be honest, in the past, I have often found my discussions with evangelicals to leave me feeling disconnected and unseen.

But, my goodness, Tovah is different. We actually share a lot of similar viewpoints about humanity. The love that shines through this woman is evident and keeps me connected with her despite our differences. Sometimes we simply agree to disagree.

Tovah arrives for the interview lugging a big foldable wooden sign with hand-painted flowers and a biblical verse on it. In her other hand is a bowl of small glass stones.

With her short and curly silver hair, Tovah looks a lot like my Grandma Ruth did when she was in her seventies.

"I told you I was going to bring the sign," she says. Hearing her New York accent always makes me feel like I'm in the presence of one of my old Jewish relatives from when I was small.

"Oh, let me get your picture!" I say. We set her sign up beside the outdoor loveseat. She sits herself down beside it, and I snap a few photos. I help Tovah load her sign back in the car, and we find a quiet place inside to do the interview.

I begin: "What brings you to this area of the world?"

"Well, I've always wanted to do a gospel outreach but never knew how to start. I prayed about it, and I got kind of a download in my brain that said, 'Go to the picnic tables at the beach and bring a cooler, and ice, and some iced tea, and cups.' It's kind of like a hospitality ministry. You offer cold drinks for people who are visiting the beach, and [they] don't have to buy anything. It's for free.

"So, I found a couple of friends. Pia was doing evangelism already, so I said, 'She's a good person, so I can maybe learn some things from her.' And she had a friend, Irma. Irma and Pia would come up from the Daytona area. We would work together from noon to two, offering cold iced tea for free and talking to people, finding out where they're from, and praying for whatever needs they might have.

"[People] ask, 'Why are you guys doing this?' And we say, 'Well, it's because we have the love of Jesus in us, and we want to share that with other people.' That might lead to discussions on spiritual things. Some people accepted faith in Him and we would baptize them in the ocean."

"You'll do that? Like, right then and there?" I ask, completely curious.

"Right then and there," she confirms.

"You don't have to have, like, a certain degree or anything to baptize people?"

"No. No, you don't. The faith would have never gotten off the ground if you needed certificates to do the things that the Apostles did."

I laugh.

Tovah continues, "I mean, they just went out there and they did it and they told people about Jesus and they shared and tried to minister to them and pray for healing.

"That's another thing—we pray for people to be healed of various afflictions. One lady I prayed for, she had the tremors from Parkinson's really badly. I mean, she had coffee and it was going everywhere, spilling all over. And I started to rebuke it. That means to tell it to stop it.

"So, through the Holy Spirit, I said, 'Stop! Stop! Stop shaking now,' over and over again. It didn't stop completely, but it radically reduced."

"Really?" I ask.

"Yes. Radically reduced to a little hand wiggle here and there.

"And now we're doing cross pennies, which is a copper penny taken out of circulation. We don't damage real currency. There's a guy in Texarkana who sells them. He gets the pennies, and then he has a hole puncher that punches out a cross. He'll give you the little cross punch-outs for free, and we glue them on little, pretty stones. Or I give them away as kitchen magnets. Sometimes I'll walk around the cars and put one on the car door for a little protection. I give them out during Bike Week and put them on the motorcycles and stuff like that.

"We've been doing this since 2017, and now I have new workers to help me. Pia and Irma stay closer to where they live because it's a *schlep* to come up to Flagler."

I smile when I hear Tovah use the Yiddish word *schlep*. It's fun to see cultures merge.

"We just try to share with people and pray for them and bless them in any way that we can. Because that's what Jesus did. You know, if you want people to see Him, they have to see Him in you first. Otherwise, it's just *words.* And, you know, you can go on YouTube and hear words."

"So you want people to *feel* it?" I ask.

"Right. Exactly. I make it very personal. I try to make people laugh. Sometimes, if someone seems a little apprehensive to take my little gift, I say, 'I know what you're thinkin'. It looks like grandma escaped from the attic again.'"

We both laugh.

"So it can really be a lot of fun. I make it very personal by taking the coin or the penny or the little stone [or] glass bead, and I take their hand and—literally—I'm *pressing on it* while I'm talking to them. It makes *an impression,* so to speak."

She continues, "And I tell them, 'Don't forget what it means. It means he suffered and died on the cross to pay for all your sins.'"

"So what do you do with people like me?" I ask Tovah. "I mean, this is an interesting conversation we're having, because you know I don't follow your faith. You know I…" I stammer for the right words.

"You have your own path," Tovah says.

"Exactly. I have my own path," I say. "So what do you do with people who come up to you and have their own path?"

"Well, we tell them that we believe the only truth about who God [is] found in the Holy Bible. And there were a lot of prophecies made that all came true that can't be denied. And, you know, they either believe it or they don't. You know, that happens.

"I had an encounter with an atheist one time, recently. He said, 'Well, I'm an atheist.' 'Oh really?' I said, and I pointed to the sky and the beach and said, 'Well, where did all this come from?' And he said, 'Chemical reactions.' And I'm like, 'Hmm, chemical reactions. Okay…so where did the chemicals come from?' And there were crickets. He didn't say a thing.

"I'm reading a book called *Tactics*. *Tactics* is about how to counter when people come with various objections. It's like a training manual, because sometimes I can draw a blank. I'm not such an expert, but this book is very helpful.

"That's why I have a t-shirt. It says 'Jesus changed my life. Ask me how.' So it's a walking billboard. I wear all these different message t-shirts. I have one that says 'Don't mess with me. I'm Jesus' trophy wife.'"

"That's so *you,* Tovah!" I laugh.

"I wear them when I go to the supermarket, and people run up to me and say, 'That's so funny. Where did you get that shirt?' And I say, 'I designed it myself.' I forgot the name of the website, but you can go there and get a mug, make a hat, or make a t-shirt.

"Sometimes nobody talks to me, but I know they see it. I'm okay if they think, 'Oh, there's that crazy lady that comes to Publix every Friday.'"

Tovah and I laugh together, and I'm reminded how much I like hanging out with her.

"Okay, Tovah, I want to switch topics, if you're okay with that, because you've got other good life stories. I don't have the Woodstock story recorded. Will you share that?" I ask, knowing it didn't fit much with the A1A theme, but it's one of my favorite stories she tells and I wanted to hear it again.

"Oh, Woodstock…" Tovah says.

"Yes! Will you tell it?" I ask.

"Sure, sure. I'll be glad to tell that story."

"Okay, so it's 1969. I have this friend at work, when I worked at RCA records. Her name was Marguerite. And Woodstock was coming to Upstate New York, and everybody was going crazy, and we bought tickets.

"So the weekend came, and we piled into my little blue Corvair. I had just bought a sleeping bag at some sporting goods store in New York City. I also packed some food. I had [a can of] little niblet corn and Vienna sausages."

"How old were you?" I ask

"I was probably twenty-three. So we get in the car. Everybody's excited. And as we're on the thruway, we see all the freaks coming from every corner of the country. They're hanging out of the cars, and they're like, 'Hey, we're going too. See you there.' And we're waving back. It was like a big party. And we finally come to the exit to get off, and then things start to slow down, and we're crawling and crawling, and there's a little bit of rain splattering. And then I look ahead, and there's some hippie chick coming up through some sunroof, doing her best

Grace Slick imitation, singing 'White Rabbit.'"

"Seriously? Was she good at it?"

"Eh, I guess. Maybe in her mind. We drove for a while. We didn't know how much further we had to go. We found an opening in a field, and we turned off for the night. We weren't going to sleep outdoors because it was raining. So imagine trying to sleep in a Corvair. We didn't get much sleep because there was a VW bus, the *ultimate* party vehicle, right next to us and they must have brought a record machine—you know, a turntable.

"They're playing records all night. Their music was in my head, and I was having dreams that The Doors were playing, even though they weren't even there. And I'm going, 'Oh, Marguerite, we've gotta get up. Come on. The concert's started. The Doors are on. The concert's started.'

"So we woke up the next day, and we had some of the corn and the Vienna sausages. I [had] brought a can opener. I drained off the niblet-corn liquid. So we had something in our stomachs, and we headed out on the road."

Tovah then describes what the concert looked like when they arrived. "We walked maybe about a mile, and as we're walking, everybody in front of us was smoking marijuana. You didn't even have to have your own because the secondhand smoke was wafting towards you. You're kind of feeling a little…kind of good, like 'Yeah. Yeah.'

And then we get to the fairgrounds, and it was just this sea of humanity, and the mud, and people were dancing with arms flailing around, wearing bandanas on their heads and top hats with a feather in it. And [there were] little kids, and frisbees were flying, and dogs were barking, and it was just, you know, what you thought it would be. It was like Hippieland."

"Now, were you guys hippies?" I ask.

"In a manner. Maybe not like the others. I don't know. I guess, in a minor way."

"How do you define 'hippie?'" I ask.

"Someone who's anti-establishment. So just smoking weed helped qualify you for that, listening to rock music, hanging out with people, talking, listening to music. To me that was Hippieville.

"So anyway, we're walking around, and the hard part was trying to find a toilet that wasn't overflowing. That's a health hazard, you know. So I went from Port-a-John to Port-a-John and finally found one I could 'use,' to put it delicately.

"So we're feeling tired. We didn't get good sleep. I'm not sure if there was music playing. I think if there was music playing, it would have pumped us up and would have made us want to stay for what was coming next. But we wanted to sleep more, we wanted more food, and we were starting to feel like we didn't want to stay—because all we could see was more of the same, even though that might not have been true.

"Marguerite had this new boyfriend back in the city, and she was thinking about her lovey-dovey boyfriend, and she missed him and all that. So she kind of pushed me towards the edge to leave. So we left early.

"The sad part is, when I tell people that I went to Woodstock, they get all excited, like they want to know 'Who did you see?' and I don't have anything to really report."

I'm smiling as I listen. I love hearing Tovah's story because I've always had such an idealistic view of Woodstock. But Tovah's story humanizes it and puts it in perspective.

"But despite of all that," Tovah continues, "I did observe many wonderful things. How peaceful the people were. Yeah, no fights, no violence. Babies were born. Somebody died. It was like a city."

Tovah goes on to reflect about her current life. "So I'm just bumping along here in my life, doing what I do, and I try live the best I can and be the best person I can."

"What's your hope for the next generations?" I ask.

"That they do the same, being your best person now. I really hope that everybody comes to…you know…it's a built-in thing with me now…that I hope everybody comes to faith and follows the principles of the scriptures. It's about being good and kind and generous and forgiving and being patient, especially with difficult people. Some people say, 'I'll only put up with so much.' Well, Jesus put up with *a lot.*"

I laugh. I may have been raised Jewish, but I've studied the Christian religion enough to know the stories.

"Sorry I'm laughing," I say, "But yeah, I think he put up with a lot."

Tovah jokes, "Yeah, he cornered the market on that one!" She pauses. "So I think, what if everyone chose him as a role model and tries to emulate him? What would the world look like?"

She pauses again. "I know this seems very narrow," she continues, "but it's where I am now. I can't go beyond that because no matter what you try, sooner or later it may fall apart and you have to retry something else. Living this way, according to God's ways, is an adventure. It doesn't seem that way to some people, but it's an adventure. It's challenging. It's filled with blessings. Even though you may endure some trials, there's always blessings.

There's people who love you."

After I stop the recorder, Tovah tells me she has one more thing to tell me. I start the recording again.

She explains that at her age, she's starting to reflect and prepare for her death. "I've put you on my contact sheet. When I go, I'd like you to reach out to all the writers from our group and let them know."

"Absolutely," I tell her. "I'd be honored."

Hope in the Wilderness
Gospel Message Outreach
tovahsez@gmail.com

July 1st, 2024

Becky's Journal

My Father's Guru

I am back home now, working on Tovah's portion of the story, and I'm crying, yet again! This is becoming a theme.

There's something I haven't mentioned yet, but as I write this, I feel like I must. My father passed away just six months ago. I am writing this book, in many ways, in honor of him, who as a psychiatrist, and just a really good human, had a knack for putting people at ease.

One of my earliest memories is a trip we took to Atlantic City around 1976. I was barely four years old. My dad's plan was to bring us to visit his ninety-two-year-old grandfather, my great-grandfather, and record an interview with him.

I remember Zayde (Yiddish for grandpa) had an apartment on one of the top floors of a high-rise building with views of the Atlantic Ocean. From that vantage point, I could see the tiny white-capped waves breaking down below.

Zayde was the oldest person I had ever met. His skin was leathery and spotted, his jowls hung loose, and he spoke with a thick Yiddish accent. He had worked hard all his life, running a small mom-and-pop grocery store in Scranton, Pennsylvania, through the Great Depression while, with my great-grandma Bubbe, raising eight kids.

When we arrived at Zayde's apartment, I think my parents might have been concerned that it would be scary for me to meet someone so old, but instead, like my dad, I felt honored to be in his presence. It was as if we had traveled hundreds of miles to meet my father's guru. Even as a very little girl, I understood the significance of this encounter.

On the day of our visit, my dad brought his tape recorder. He set it up with a microphone and began the interview with his grandpa.

I realize as I write to you that this small event was seminal in my life. It was perhaps my first introduction to the power of listening with an open heart. Unknowingly, I got to observe my dad and my great-grandfather cultivating a sacred space together. I was witnessing firsthand my dad's greatest skill. Together they were making a deep and holy connection.

I believe on that day a very special kind of love began to wiggle its way into my four-year-old body. It has made an impression on me for a lifetime. To this day, this is why I do what I do.

Unfortunately, my mother and I haven't had the same sort of relationship. My mother has struggled with mental health issues for most of her life due to her own difficult childhood. She was, and still is, a spritely, playful, highly creative woman who can be very fun to be around. But sometimes, when she is not careful, her unresolved childhood wounds seep out into our world.

As a child, I felt a great responsibility for her pain, although it probably had nothing to do with me. Some of the unhealthy patterns I notice within myself and in my relationships with others are rooted, I believe, in my own unresolved wounds.

Now as I work to become a healthier, more whole human in this world, I have chosen to separate temporarily from her both physically and emotionally as a way for me to better understand and heal the broken parts of myself. This choice I have made for temporary separation has been difficult and grueling. It weighs heavy on me. What a strange thing to love someone so much but also know space is needed.

I realize some of the content I'm adding to this book does not have much to do with A1A, and maybe I'm divulging too much, but I made a vow upon starting this writing journey that I would be real with you.

Perhaps it's through these people I speak with, through the doorways we open in our hearts as we talk, that I am rekindling the love I felt between me and my father. Maybe, also, it's helping me better understand the strain between myself and my mother. Maybe it's helping me forgive myself, and her, and rewrite the stories of my past.

Hopefully, you're learning something too.

Ironically, as I was meditating at the beach yesterday, sending imaginary waves of love out to my mother, I got a surprise text from the next person on my list to interview. Her name is Ellen—my mother's name as well.

Ellen had invited me to meet some of the folks who live in Surfside Estates, a senior-living community in Beverly Beach just a few miles north of Flagler Beach. She's offered me a tour and a golf-cart ride. I'm excited to see what I will learn.

Ellen Karp-Bendana

Surfside Estates
Beverly Beach, Florida
July 1st, 2024

Golf-Cart Escapades

I drive along A1A into Beverly Beach, a tiny community just a few miles north of Flagler Beach. Following my GPS, I wander down the narrow paved roads of Surfside Estates. I pass row after row of tightly placed mobile homes or, as they're more commonly called now, "manufactured homes."

The stereotype of a trailer park that was ingrained in me from early in my life disappears completely as I drive through Surfside Estates. Each home is carefully cared for, each one kept up with its own unique landscaping and small but well-manicured lawn.

I pull into Ellen's driveway and knock on her door. She greets me, and I'm instantly struck by her effervescent personality. She invites me in and gives me a tour of her home. We sit down in her kitchen for a bit, swap stories, and then head to her carport and climb in the golf cart.

I precariously hop into the passenger side and notice Ellen has already turned the cart on and is ready to go. I do my best to set up the lapel mics as Ellen pulls out fast, driving right through her back yard, and I feel more like I'm on a ride at Disney World than driving through a senior-living community.

"So this is a resident-owned cooperative," she says as we zip down the road. "This park has been here since the late '70s. Originally, it was owned by the gentleman who owns Camptown Resort, but in the late '80s, the residents said, 'Let's see if we can try to take control of our own destiny.' So this was one of the first resident-owned cooperatives in the State of Florida," Ellen says proudly. "At that time, everybody pitched in $25,000 to buy their share. There's two hundred and thirty-nine homes in here, and we wrote a check for six million dollars.

"Because it's a resident-owned cooperative and we're not for profit, we have HOA dues, but they're really designed to just cover the expenses."

We turn onto a longer road that spans the length of the neighborhood and butts up against the Matanzas River.

"As you can see, we're right on the Intracoastal." Pointing out a small strip of green marshland that sits between the river and the road, she says, "This land is part of the Army Corp of Engineers. It can't be developed, so we get to enjoy the beautiful water view on this side, which not a lot of people realize is back here."

We turn the corner again, and I hold on tight.

"I bought my home two weeks before Hurricane Matthew. Since I've been here, almost eight years, there's been forty-five new homes put in. And the biggest change is…"

Ellen interrupts herself to wave down a few neighbors walking their dogs.

"Hey, Marcy! How are you?" she calls out to two ladies in a yard. "This is Becky. Becky's writing a book about A1A, and if you're interested, we're going to be up on 'the perch' at seven if you want to participate. I'd love for her to meet as many residents as possible."

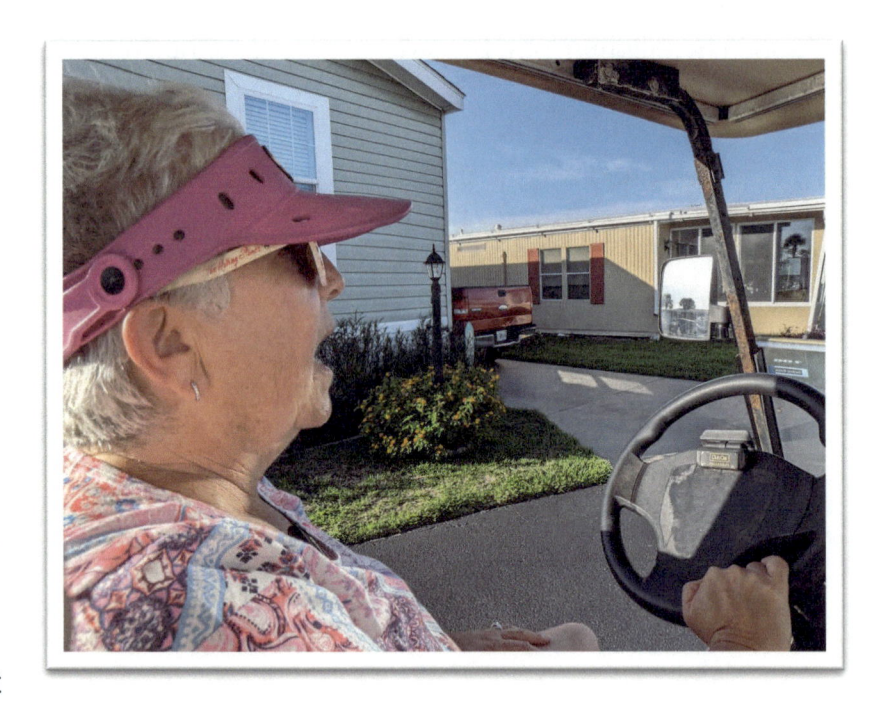

Marcy smiles and nods, and Ellen continues to drive. I take a quick photo of her.

"We're kind of like a family. Everybody sort of knows each other. The park's big enough that it's not overwhelming. You know your neighbors. I'd say seventy percent of [the] people live here full time and thirty percent are snowbirds."

At this point, I've completely lost my bearings. Each street looks pretty much the same to me. And so, I try to focus on Ellen's words as we zoom past the many homes.

"There's been a dramatic improvement with the new homes that came in, unfortunately because of the hurricanes. The biggest problem with this park is the flooding that we get from the Intracoastal."

She points out a series of older homes that rest low to the ground.

"When the wind blows, as you know, it doesn't let the Intracoastal recede, and then we get water about halfway up the park. And that's what has caused a lot of these new homes [to be built]."

Ellen slows down again to speak to another neighbor. "Hey, Jan. This is Becky Magnolia. She's writing a book on A1A. If you're around, we're going to meet up on the perch."

Awkwardly, I smile and wave, not quite sure how I feel about the temporary celebrity status I've been given.

"If someone wants to put a new home in here," Ellen continues, "you can't just go to a manufactured-home dealer and buy something off a lot and say, 'Oh yeah, I got a great deal.' It has to be custom ordered and built to what they call 'Wind Zone Exposure D.'"

Ellen waves to another neighbor.

"Because we're so close to the coast, [the homes] have to be built with two-by-sixes every four feet. The new ones are built to sustain one-hundred-thirty-mile-an-hour winds. They have hurricane straps built into the trusses that go over the roof."

After arriving at the clubhouse and giving me a tour of the library and exercise facilities, Ellen brings me up to the roof. On one side of 'the perch,' we can see A1A. Behind the RV park across the street is a view of the beach.

Several residents are already waiting for us when we arrive, so we sit at a table and everyone introduces themselves.

As the sun sets over the Intracoastal, the group exchanges happy stories with me about how they each discovered Surfside Estates, sharing their love and pride for their unique, cozy community.

July 3rd, 2024

Becky's Journal

Angels in the Sky

The air was hot when I arrived at Ragga Surf Cafe on Wednesday. The slight breeze off the ocean was the only reprieve from the beating sun. When my friend Courtney approached the food truck, I noticed she didn't quite have that Courtney-shine I was used to seeing.

We ordered lunch and sat at a table. For some reason, intuitively I knew not to turn on the mics. At that moment, I needed a friend more than I needed just another interview under my belt. Turns out she did too.

Courtney used to work at Java Joint. She was a manager there before the establishment changed owners. We got to know each other well over the years when I would come by to eat breakfast and write.

I had reached out to Courtney to see if she wanted to be part of my project, thinking maybe we could recount some stories from the restaurant. But as we were catching up on our current lives, in passing, she mentioned that her father had died one month earlier. Because I feel these things shouldn't be just passed over, I began asking her questions about him. Apparently, they were very close. As she talked, she became a bit choked up, and I could tell behind her sunglasses she was crying. She apologized.

"Don't worry. Crying is always welcome with me," I told her. "I cry all the time!"

She then told me a beautiful story about her drive back to Florida after being up north to say her final goodbyes to her father. She had been on I95 for hours and decided in a quick decision to turn off and take A1A. Something drew her to Marineland. In her sorrow, hoping for some sort of resolution and peace, she went to the beach. There, in the distance over the ocean, she saw a small rain cloud, and from it, a rainbow appeared. As she described, "It was shaped like two angel wings." To Courtney, this was the confirmation she needed.

Since her father's passing, she's found a multitude of sea glass on the beaches in both browns and greens. She says the colors make her think of her father's hazel eyes.

We both agreed that there's something very special about Marineland. Neither of us could place it, but we both felt it.

Some days, I feel like grief is in the air. It swarms around us, and yet we all go about our lives like loss is not happening all the time, like we don't struggle with those deep, rich, and very real feelings of loneliness, longing, and loss.

After seeing Courtney, I came home and sank back into sadness. Sometimes I just feel like, even with so much good around me, I'm locked into my current predicaments so tightly, like a taut winding of ropes around my body. The more I try to break out, the tighter they squeeze.

Feeling the depth of darkness start to drag me down, I decide to boil a kettle of water and make myself the sample of Joyful Tea that Denise had given me.

As the tea steeped, I pulled out my phone and purchased an audiobook I've had my eye on: *The Places That Scare You: A Guide to Fearlessness in Difficult Times*.

The teachings of the great Buddhist teacher Pema Chödrön soon filled my kitchen, and I began cleaning the house. As I rigorously mopped the floor, Pema talked about the bravery it takes to look at life head-on, to observe and note each flicker of emotion and thought that percolates in our bodies.

As I work on my own book, I realize I am working through my grief—not just of losing my father, but grieving the old me, the loss of the young suburban mother and wife who crossed that bridge fourteen years ago. It sounds funny, but some days, I still grieve the loss of that pampered Jewish hippie princess I once was. It's still me in many ways, but I am changing. I am becoming something unknown and new.

As terrifying as that can feel, at times, I'm learning that with change also comes a new, exciting way of being. Through each of these interviews, I'm learning a new kind of love. I'm learning how it feels to find *kinship* in everyone I meet, how it feels to become a new person, one who loves fully with boldness and curiosity.

* * *

I checked my blood pressure today. It's high. I feel as if it's connected to the striving I do…that constant sense of running I feel, grabbing at an elusive goal I suspect is actually already here, waiting for me in the corners of my life. It is love itself, waiting for me to come back home.

July 4th, 2024
Becky's Journal

It's the evening of the Fourth of July. The Inlet Store was crazy busy today. Ellen had invited me to join the retirees at Surfside Estates for a cookout. As much as I loved the idea, after work I was tired. So I decided to spend the evening of the Fourth of July alone.

Over the past month, I've continued to post my progress on this book on Facebook, and apparently, people are taking note. Midway through the day today, an exuberant older woman came into the store and introduced herself as Kim. She explained that she had been following my stories and that her niece was in town and she "just knew" we had to meet.

Harmony was about my age, standing to one side of the register, propping herself up with a walking cane. She looked a bit weak, like perhaps she was recovering from a serious illness. This made me curious. I could tell she had some good stories to tell, and for some reason, I felt connected to her right away. When she told me she was a psychic medium, I knew we had to talk. Occasionally I've been known to work as a professional tarot card reader. Apparently we had a lot in common, so we exchanged numbers.

Three days later, I met her at Debra Jean's and we talked over coffee. We both agreed it felt like we were old sisters, finally, after lifetimes, reuniting. After talking for over an hour, I learned her story of a debilitating illness that had left her bedridden. She was now recovering and returning to the world. She would soon be headed back to her home in Atlanta, but I knew I had found a friend. Hopefully we will meet again.

Harmony James
A Luminous Heart
www.aluminousheart.com

July 5th, 2024

Becky's Journal

Kayak Therapy

In the book *The Places That Scare You,* Pema Chödrön says–and I paraphrase–f something isn't working, do something different. And so today, still struggling with some deep and angsty moods, I did something different. Very different.

I arrived at Bing's Landing in The Hammock around 8:45 in the morning. AyoLane was already there with two bright-orange kayaks already unloaded from his trailer.

I'll admit it. I was anxious. The brackish Matanzas River is connected to the ocean, so tides come in and tides go out. The back swampland is riddled with oyster beds and a vast and mysterious labyrinth of mangroves. As I've heard, you can get easily lost or stuck there if you don't time your journey with the tides.

But I knew AyoLane enough from our previous conversation to know there was no one I'd trust more to be kayaking with in the winding unknown.

Our travel companion for the day, Darby, AyoLane's friend, arrived full of spirit and spunk, clearly ready for an adventure. After our brief introductions, I carefully climbed into the kayak and AyoLane pushed me off into the river.

No longer attached to the land, I experienced what I can only describe as a small freak-out. In a flash, I pictured myself being swept into the current and being sent off helplessly into the unknown, but I played it cool. I would be in charge of that vehicle for the next two hours, and it was up to me to take control. With a bit of maneuvering, I started to regain my confidence. Darby came out behind me, and I felt my nerves calm. I wasn't alone.

And so, the three of us set off across the Matanzas River, past the speeding boats and jet skis, through a gap in the other side of the riverway that opened up into marshland. Along the edges of this watery terrain, mangrove sprouts stood like small muddy men being born from the rich, earthy sediment. In the distance, sparse palms and dead oaks dotted the horizon.

With the main riverway disappearing in the distance, I felt my whole body settle. Aside from a few crab traps, there were no other signs of humans.

As we rounded the bend, an osprey with a silvery fish in its claws landed in a nearby tree. Rather than forging ahead, the three of us stopped and together admired the majestic bird as he stretched his wings out wide and began to tear into his lunch.

I noticed my mind and my feelings were still somewhat tied up with the emotions I had clung to back at home, but remembering the mindfulness teachings I have studied, I acknowledged those emotions, and we continued on.

As we paddled, the narrow waterway opened up into a big lake encircled by golden and leathery green mangroves. We paused once again and felt the beauty of the space.

"This is the source of life," AyoLane said. "Each droplet of water contains thousands of life forms within it." I could feel it—this space of rebirth.

As we paddled, we took turns talking about our lives, exchanging the names of all the great spiritual books we each had read. AyoLane told us the story of receiving his name. AyoLane, a Lakota name, is difficult to translate into English. In simplest terms it means

"Yellow Hawk," but as he explained, this translation doesn't do it justice. I believe, from what he told me, its meaning could be more closely interpreted to mean "protector" or "provider."

We paddled on and continued to talk about life. Every now and then, I'd sink back into my sad and chattering mind. But with these two new friends, surrounded by the waters, the feelings didn't last, and I began to feel myself become raw and present with these people I barely knew.

We arrived back at Bing's Landing about two hours later and hungry, so we headed over to Captain's BBQ, just a short walk away. A long line of people were packed into the small space. So we grabbed our food, and I lead Darby and AyoLane outside to one of my favorite secret picnic tables beneath the trees. We ate good food and talked, and talked some more.

I am home now, typing up my notes and feeling what I can only describe as an ancient sense of calm. It's a stillness in my soul, a settling, a peace. It's as if the waters themselves have worked their way beneath my skin.

As I rest here, I can feel this nameless sense of aliveness within me, breathing with the serenity of a sleeping baby, my body rising and falling effortlessly with each breath.

During our outing, I had told Darby and AyoLane the story of how I got my last name—Magnolia. During the several years that I followed the Bhakti path of Hinduism, I had yearned for a spiritual name. But early on, I had decided I couldn't just give myself a name. It had to be given to me by some sort of guru. However, that magical, perfect teacher never came.

Instead, I realized, that guru, the teacher, was not going to come to me in the form of some long-bearded guy in robes. In fact, I instinctively knew the guru wasn't going to show up in the form of a single person at all but instead arrive within *every* person I met. It was going to come to me through *life itself*, through every situation I encountered.

So rather than receiving my name from some holy man on a hill, it seemed quite reasonable that I'd end up receiving my name in an everyday, not-so-magical way. For me, as it happened, I got my name at a garage sale.

I was at an estate sale on the Matanzas River in The Hammock. I had just bought a couch for my new home, but I needed to get my friend to help me transport it with his truck. I paid for the couch and told the homeowner, "My name is Becky." I then gestured towards A1A. "I'll be right back. I live just down the road on Magnolia."

When I returned to the garage sale, they were packing up, but I found the couch still there, with a piece of paper resting on it. On the paper, it said simply, "Becky Magnolia." The moment I saw the paper, I knew *this* was my name. Somehow, being named unintentionally by a woman at a garage sale seemed the perfectly imperfect way for me to be named.

And so it stuck. I had found my new last name.

On the water today, AyoLane told us about the great Lakota ceremonies he had attended. He described the heartfelt awakening the attendees experienced these sacred events. But, he said, sometimes after such a spiritual opening, when one returned to their ordinary life, an experience of grief would occur.

Although I haven't been part of a lot of intense spiritual gatherings, I do know the feelings of separation I've felt after opening wide to the realm of the spirit and then being dropped back into the "ordinary" world.

In order to preserve and cherish the beauty of the ceremony before leaving the event, AyoLane told us, the elders would symbolically take the experience and "wrap it in red," as if securing the experience with tenderness and love in a blanket, protecting its grace from the elements, so when one returned to the land of the everyday, the wrapped-in-red "package" would retain its preciousness.

He explained that whenever one wanted to revisit the magic of the event, they could "unwrap the red" and share it with whomever they wished to pass it on with love. This would provide an opportunity to not only share the sacred moment, but allow it to flourish and grow.

As I write to you right now, in the stillness of the evening, I feel as if I am unwrapping the red so you, the reader, can experience the holiness of the many sacred moments I have encountered on my writing journey thus far. I hope you can feel, in your own way, the peace we felt when we were out on the water today. Perhaps this entire book is an unwrapping, a sharing, with you, my reader-friend, the experience of the sacredness, the holiness I have felt sitting with these people I meet on my path.

July 7th, 2024

Becky's Journal

A Message from Dad

This morning, I went for a walk. Taking a new path, I ended up in an abandoned parking lot near the Hammock Dunes Bridge. The original builders of the property had left many of the old oaks. Unstoppable in their magnitude and growth, the trees have flourished, outliving the former structures that have since been torn down, their thick roots busting through the old concrete.

I settled under an ancient tree that was draped in Spanish moss and noticed three palms in front of me, presumably planted decades ago. As I sat there, I began feeling a strange sense of longing, a homesickness for a place that wasn't anywhere in particular, but something, somehow I knew in my heart. Maybe it was that indescribable longing AyoLane talked about, the grief of knowing a spiritual home and then losing it.

I hoped for some sort of answer, some purpose to my momentary upwelling of emotion, but it never fully came, so I stood up and started heading home. But as I was walking away, I felt an internal calling to return to the parking lot.

In the past few years, I've made a commitment to listen to my "inner guide," so in responding to this tug, I turned back to the lot, put on my favorite musical playlist, and started dancing. The second song was by Jason Mraz, "I'm Yours."

In time with the music, I felt my body lift. I began to spin, liberating the tight places within me. A smile came onto my face and then, just as the song ended, I turned around and discovered a hawk feather standing upright, wedged in a crack in the concrete. I felt as if it had been placed there just for me.

I feel a shift lately. In place of sadness is a warmth within my soul. It seems this simple act of letting life dictate its course brings me to just what I need. It's a strange and magical thing.

That morning I walked back home with Jason Mraz's lyrics in my head:

> "I've been spending way too long checking my tongue in the mirror
> And bending over backwards just to try to see it clearer
> But my breath fogged up the glass
> And so I drew a new face and I laughed
> I guess what I be saying is there ain't no better reason
> To rid yourself of vanities and just go with the seasons
> It's what we aim to do
> Our name is our virtue"

In the afternoon I headed to work. Around 2:00 p.m., an older gentleman came in with whom I assume was his family. With them was a young girl in braids, maybe eleven years old. She spoke to me confidently with a foreign accent I couldn't quite place.

We hear many accents here along A1A—Puerto Rican, Dominican, Portuguese, Russian, Polish—but I couldn't quite place hers. My best guess was she was visiting from a Scandinavian country.

The older gentleman, tall and clean-cut, wandered back to the cooler with his younger friend to find some beers. The girl and her mom eventually left the store, leaving the two men behind. A few minutes later the men arrived at the counter with two tall, twenty-ounce cans of beer.

The friend spoke to me in broken English: "I want it bigger."

I looked at the can and then at him. When I realized he was making fun of the large can size, I laughed.

"Americans are serious about their beer," I joked.

"Oh, we are too," the older gentleman said.

"What language are you guys speaking?" I asked.

"Danish," he answered.

We continued joking and making small talk. The older gentleman asked me my name. His English was much better than his traveling companion's.

I then asked him his name.

"Søren," he said.

"How do you spell that?" I asked.

As he spelled it out, "S-O-R-E-N," I wrote it down on a piece of paper. He explained it meant "son of" and proceeded to explain its link to his father's name.

After chatting a bit more, he said, "It was nice to meet you, Becky. We will be back soon!" As the two men left, they raised their beers in the air as if they were toasting to their upcoming beach adventure. I waved goodbye.

About an hour later, Søren returned. He and his friend wandered the shop until he found a light-blue baseball cap with the words "Matanzas Inlet" on it. It's one of our best sellers. He put it on and smiled big, like he had found life's perfection in this little cap. He walked up to the counter.

"This is the perfect hat," he said.

My heart warmed, seeing this man so happy with such a silly, simple item. We chatted for a few more minutes, and the two men left.

About half an hour passed, and they returned once again. This time, Søren made a beeline for the hats and returned to the counter with two more matching ones.

I laughed.

"The family wants them now!" he said.

"So are these hats going back to Denmark?" I asked.

"No, actually I live in Madison, Wisconsin."

I lit up. "Madison!? That's where I'm from," I said.

In my fourteen years in Florida, I've only met maybe four people from my hometown.

"I live on the Westside," he said. "I'm from a neighborhood called Tamarack."

"I know it well!" I said, and a rush of childhood memories came to me: bike rides to work as a teen, Girl Scout meetings at my friends' houses, visits to the pool, playing tennis at the club.

But then it hit me. I had a more recent connection to Tamarack Trails.

Speaking now with a bit less levity, I told Søren, "My father… He's buried in the cemetery that backs up into Tamarack Trails. He died six months ago. The houses in Tamarack are just feet away from my father's burial plot."

Another flash of memory came to me. At the funeral, between tears, I was able to joke with my childhood neighbor and friend, Abby, who had joined me graveside that day. We thought it was funny that my dad's final resting place was to be in our childhood stomping grounds, Tamarack Trails.

Søren and I smiled and celebrated together this synchronistic moment, and once again, he and his friend left.

There was a lull in customers, giving me a chance to really feel into this serendipitous event. I thought of Mom…I thought of Dad…and then, not even five minutes later, the two men returned.

This time, they didn't get a beer. They didn't go back to the hats. Instead, they came right to the counter.

"We have something to show you, Becky," Søren said. His tone was not playful anymore. Without words, Søren gestured towards his friend who was holding his cell phone up to me. I leaned forward over the counter to see a single photo on display. It was an image of the little girl in braids I had met earlier. She was with a friend, sitting on a marble bench. Engraved on it, I could make out the word "LOVE." Then, looking closer, I noticed the background. A cemetery. My Dad's cemetery, with the telltale row of Tamarack houses behind it.

What were the odds of him having that picture in his phone?

At that point, there was no use in holding back the tears. I began to cry, uncontrollably. I had immediately been transported to the graveside. I was back in that spot, two thousand miles away from A1A, saying goodbye to Dad all over again.

Without hesitation, Søren walked behind the counter and wrapped me in his big arms. It had been a very long time since I had had a hug from anyone. I cried some more, and this stranger, now friend, embraced me for a long time. He gently rubbed my back, soothing me. And all of my heartbreak, my sorrows, my fears, my shame melted into the safety of this stranger's arms.

The world now blurry with tears, I looked at him. We just smiled at each other. "This world is beautiful, Becky. There are so many good people."

I don't know what moved him to say those words, but they were exactly what I needed to hear.

"Thank you," I said, and the two men left. I never saw them again.

In Jewish tradition, after a burial, it is customary to hold what is called a "minion." This is a sacred gathering after the funeral where a group of people come together and pray, usually at the mourner's house.

During our stay in Madison after my dad's death, we had rented a huge hundred-year-old farmhouse with enough rooms to house myself, my brothers, their families, Abby, her brother, and her mother, Mrs. Winger. Mrs. Winger, as we all still call her, was like a second mother to me growing up.

In the evening after the funeral, the rabbi came to the house. We moved chairs from the other room into a circle in the parlor. We said the mourner's Kaddish, the prayer for the dead, and went around the circle, telling stories about Dad. As we talked, his presence was palpable. Together, we rekindled his soul.

I shyly muttered to Mrs. Winger, who sat beside me, "I feel like singing." My family is not a singing family, but I was feeling an ache to sing the mourner's Kaddish.

Mrs. Winger nudged me with her arm. "Speak up," she said, and so I asked the rabbi if he'd mind leading us in the song. He happily obliged, and together we sang.

Mrs. Winger nudged me again. "Do you have any more songs?" she asked me quietly. Again I felt the pull, but I was embarrassed to even mention the song as it wasn't a Jewish song at all but a silly kids' song from my days when I'd watch Sesame Street as a kid with Dad.

"Could we sing 'Who Are the People in Your Neighborhood?'" I asked sheepishly. "It was a song Dad and I used to sing when I was little."

Everyone was happy to oblige.

And so, with love in my heart and tears in my eyes, we sang as a collective that silly little kids' song that has reverberated throughout my life.

As I write this, I'm feeling so much love for my dad, who showed me what love really meant, not just for myself but the world.

> "Oh, who are the people in your neighborhood?
> In your neighborhood
> In your neighborhood
> Oh, who are the people in your neighborhood?
> They're the people that you meet
> when you're walking down the street
> They're the people that you meet each day."

And THIS is why I write this book to you. To remind us all not just of the magic of life along A1A but in celebration of the honest and real human connections we have an opportunity to make….each day!

Whether you live in my neck of the woods or somewhere else, we are all neighbors…and this grand planet is our neighborhood.

Who are the people in our neighborhood? We are!

Although Dad never told me these truths, he didn't have to. He exemplified them in his life. And now his beautiful soul, no longer trapped in a sickened body, gets to connect with it all, with anyone and everyone he chooses.

Remember how I said that opening myself up to the Universe brings me everything I need?

I believe this is true.

Most definitely.

July 9th, 2024

Becky's Journal

Tonglen and the Art of Suffering

I'm at home, sitting again in my favorite paisley and pink chair, looking out at the river. My legs are outstretched, I'm wrapped in my favorite yellow blanket, and I am breathing.

I just listened to a chapter of *The Places That Scare You* and am trying out a Buddhist meditation called Tonglen.

In this mediation, Pema tells us to first settle ourselves. As we relax, she suggests we allow ourselves to open into a space of expansiveness, open our hearts, our pores, our *very being,* wide, gentle, and relaxed. The sensation may be fleeting, she says, but gently allow it to come.

We then begin to meditate on a person, particularly one who we believe is suffering. She suggests we don't just meditate on the person themselves but specifically on their pain, their grief, their agony. On our in-breath, we allow their pain in. We allow for the tightness, the constriction, the claustrophobia.

And then on the exhale, we release back into that sense of expansiveness, transforming the internalized suffering into pure, white light, into compassion, into delicate and airy alchemized gold.

For the first time since the river trip, I am feeling that clear calm, like that silent call of the river is resting in my heart.

As I sit here breathing in the pain of the world and releasing it as joy, tiny frogs the size of my fingernail are dropping (from what seems like the heavens) at random intervals and landing on my yoga mat on the porch. My back door is open, and I can hear their delicate bodies dropping with a soft "plunk." They sit for a moment and propel themselves outward into the bushes. I think I've counted twelve frogs now who have followed this pattern.

Drop, plunk, fly! Drop, plunk, fly!

Again and again, these baby frogs arrive and leave, like my breath—the feelings of constriction and then the release.

A baby lizard is now having a face-off with one of these tiny frogs. They appear to be a bit perplexed with each other.

How precious we all are.

* * *

I just watched a video from the 1990s. Comedian and talk show host Arsenio Hall had Mr. Rogers on as a guest. Arsenio was concerned about the state of modern media and the effect it was having on children, so he asked Mr. Rogers how we could help.

Mr. Rogers replied in his gentle voice, "Let everyone know that each one of us is precious. Let people know that we all have value in this life."

I'm crying again. :)

* * *

If my book was an improv Jazz performance, this would be part of the song where the band starts to slow down and we, as the audience, come to believe the song is about to be over.

In fact, yesterday, as I talked to my brother on the phone, I said, "I've finished the book today!" But I think there's one more section to go, two more interviews, and a few more stories to share.

PART IV

"Follow your bliss. If you do follow your bliss, you put yourself on a kind of track that has been there all the while waiting for you, and the life you ought to be living is the one you are living. When you can see that, you begin to meet people who are in the field of your bliss, and they open the doors to you. I say, follow your bliss and don't be afraid, and doors will open where you didn't know they were going to be."

–Joseph Campbell

July 14th, 2024

Becky's Journal

I woke up this morning, picked up my phone, and opened Facebook. I'm not sure what tipped me off, but I had a weird feeling something significant had just happened in the news.

I googled "Breaking News" and saw a video of former President Trump being grazed by a bullet last night in Pennsylvania. The news was vague, but the video was clear. An assassination attempt had taken place.

I reached out to my ex-husband, who in the past had always been my go-to friend when confusing, scary stuff happened in the world. We theorized about the events and pondered the outcome, and together we held space for the strange uncertainty ahead. Although, for some reason, I have trouble saying it directly to him with words, I hope he knows I'm still grateful for his presence.

Love is a very strange thing. It doesn't follow the rules we've been taught. It meanders like a river, carving out paths we can't always control, making tributaries and gorges and surprising left turns. But I suspect it is this unpredictability, this fragility, that makes it all so precious.

The working title for this book is *Local A1A*. However, as I watch the book evolve, it's earning a new name. What do you think of *The Healing of the Old Road*? AyoLane suggested this one. I feel like this land, this road, and the people who live and work here offer a kind of healing. Maybe together we each contribute something to a greater and grand healing for us all.

As I was writing this just now, my phone chimed. I opened my email to find a new message in my inbox. It's a weekly quote I receive from Tibetan Buddhist teacher Chogyam Trungpa Ripoche. The message seems to perfectly coincide with what I have just written:

"A Drop of Sanity in the Ocean of Dharma—Working together with others, individuals begin to contribute their little portion of sanity to the bigger situation. Your contribution must be just a drop of sanity, but if everybody contributes, there will be lots of drops in the ocean. And it helps. From developing personal warmth toward ourselves, we generate warmth and kindness to others in turn."

I'm not sure the gravity of yesterday's political events have sunk into me yet. The world is upturning, shifting, and changing fast. May we all step beyond the fires of fear and continue to lead our lives from the raw and delicate softness of our hearts.

Jeremie Purdy

**Debra Jean's
The Hammock, Florida**

The Writing on the Wall

It's early Tuesday morning, and Debra Jean's is closed, but owner Jeremie has told me to meet her there anyway. We enter the café from the side door, and Jeremie heads straight behind the counter to make us both coffees.

From where I sit, I can peer into the small side room, where the white walls are covered in words written in black Sharpie marker. During the several months that Debra Jean's has been open, guests have left their mark, writing a special kind of graffiti that Jeremie encourages. Along the walls are hundreds of sentences, proverbs from the Bible that customers have left when they visit.

As Jeremie starts up the espresso machine, we talk. Jeremie has a knack for diving in deep and fast with her conversations. We start off by discussing the difficulty so many of us have with being in the present moment.

"I think we are all on autopilot, which is why we get triggered so fast," Jeremie says.

She continues, "We've all kind of got into survival mode of just putting our head down and going. Because, honestly, who wants to look up sometimes?

"I've already told my staff, 'Listen, I don't care what anybody's walk of life is. I don't care what their belief system is. I don't care who they are, what they identify as. We are loving everybody the same way…We're here to love the world and to love our community."

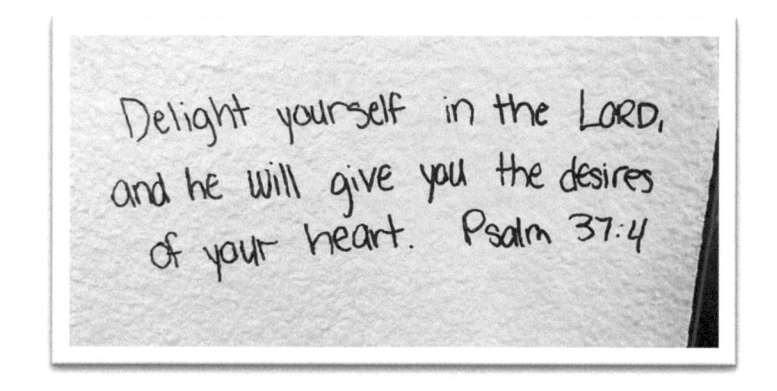

> Delight yourself in the LORD, and he will give you the desires of your heart. Psalm 37:4

I smile. I already know this conversation is going to be good.

"So what motivated you to start Debra Jean's?" I ask.

"I bought the building with my husband as an investment, really having no plan and no vision, and everybody, including my friends who are very successful financial advisors, told me, 'You're an idiot. What are you doing?'" She laughs. "But I don't get phased by things like that because I'm so strong-minded and strong-willed, and I really don't care what anybody thinks about anything, ever, usually, which is kind of a good thing and a bad thing.

"I learn lessons the hard way. That's the only way I learn. So I bought this not really having a vision other than I know that I'm from here and I love this area and I've always driven by this little building…it was hideous. Honestly, it was an eyesore. It was orange, and it just needed lots of love, and I could really see the potential. I didn't really have the vision for it yet.

"And then, my brother Kyle got all excitled. He started saying, 'Oh my gosh, I can see this…I can see that.' He called me up one day and goes, 'I don't know what you're doing, but can I be a part of it?' He was all excited. I was like, 'Sure…even though I still don't know what I'm doing.' And he said, 'Okay, I'm gonna think of some things.'

"He called me on another day and said, 'I've got it! Let's start a coffee-roasting company.' I was like, 'That's the dumbest idea I've ever heard.' And I hung up on him.

"And then, two weeks later, I was walking across my yard and I just had this vision. I could see the whole life of it. I could see the roasting part of it. I could see the people, the gathering. I wasn't so much seeing the business. I was just seeing what was needed, I guess. I just felt it so strong. I really felt God was saying, 'Listen. Here's what I want *you* to do for me. You don't need to understand why.' And from that moment, I was like a dog on a bone. Like, I just whited out. Nothing else existed. I just went into hyperfocus…I had no money to do it.

"We had already bought the building. That was a miracle alone. And so, I'm researching the cost of all this stuff. In this economy, I was not comfortable with going in and getting a loan for hundreds of thousands of dollars for equipment. And so I call my brother up.

"I said, 'All right, I'll do this, but only if we can do it organic.' I said, 'I'm not gonna open up something where we're just giving people more crap. Because we've got plenty of those around here.' And I said, 'I'm not kidding. That's the line, a hard line. It's organic, or we're not doing it.'

"So we started the coffee-roasting company first because we really wanted to have that product to sell in the café. Honestly, what this has turned into is nothing [like] what I envisioned."

"Really?" I ask.

"Yeah, it's had a life of its own. My husband and I had an investment building down in Daytona, and I had done my own renovations and contracting. We were actually doing really well on it. So we ended up selling that building, and we took those funds and bought all this stuff we needed for [the café].

"That was really a miracle…It's like what you've talked about with your book. We always go in with what we think, but I believe anything that has life to it is going to constantly evolve into what God's plan is for it.

"I tell myself all the time, 'This is not mine.' This does not belong to me. This is not yours. There's no reason for anybody to get butt hurt over mistakes or anything like that because this is not about *us*.

"I've told my staff from day one, 'I don't care about your mistakes. I care about how we're going to handle our mistakes and communicate to our customers and give them the best service that we possibly can because, yes, they're coming in here for just a cup of coffee and maybe something to eat. But we don't know what kind of day they've had.'

"We had one lady who was a nurse, and she must have been having a *very* bad day. She came in and almost threw her cake at us. But I could tell she's just having a bad day. Who throws cake? She was having a bad day.

"We don't know what anybody's walking in here with. Everybody just wants a little bit of peace and a little break from the monotony, or whatever it is they're going through, and having a really nice place, a *beautiful* place [is important]. That's why we all love art—because we create beauty, whether we know it or not. Tattoos, clothing…it's in us because our Creator loves it.

"So that was the most important thing to me. I kept joking. I was like, 'If we make it cute, they will come.'"

I laugh and say, "You've created the female version of *Field of Dreams*."

"Everybody makes fun of me. If I get a little box, I'm gonna make it the prettiest little box I can get…so [the design element] was the thing that really geeked me out. I really do love all of it but [especially] the design element and being thoughtful about it."

Jeremie points to the handcrafted wooden counter behind the coffee bar. "I brought in a lot of locals," she says. "This is [built from] a sweet gum tree. It's actually considered a trash tree around here. It was done by a local artisan. And Pete, our tile guy, grew up here. Everybody that was a part of this has been here in our community for so long and does what they do so well, so it was just a matter of bringing all that little expertise in."

Jeremie points to the trademark mural of giant flowers that spans the largest wall in the café.

"Beth and I collaborated on that. I told her basically what I was looking for and the feel I wanted to get. I mentioned my mom. Debra actually means 'bee,' and my mom's name was Debra. She loved bees and sunflowers, so [adding that bee] was actually a little surprise Beth did for me. She didn't even tell me. She just put in a little bee and little ladybug.

"Beth didn't even know that my mom loved ladybugs too. You see it hiding over there? And it was funny—the day she was painting the ladybug, we had ladybugs all over the window. It was the craziest thing.

"Little God-coincidences like that just remind me along the way. They're kind of cheering me on, saying 'You're on the right path.'"

"So tell me more about this skill you have developed for following your visions," I say.

"It's almost like being in a blank room, and all of a sudden, a TV screen comes on, and it's playing a movie of your life that you're watching. I can see it so clearly, I guess, which is why I can move so fast.

"It's not that I'm *not* terrified. I'm terrified in everything I do. I just do it anyway because I'm insane…I'm sure a few people would vouch for that," she says with a smile.

"But I just know that I have been through so much in my life, and I know that God has never failed me. I feel like I get one life, and as I age and get older, I'm more aware of how frail and precious and beautiful life really is.

"It's really not about me. It's hard to not see from our [own] perspective because we're in ourselves so much. We're constantly thinking about ourselves and, you know, having to care for ourselves. That's a survival instinct that we all have, to be like that. I probably operate eighty percent like that. It [requires] thought and consciousness to push out of that, to think outside of myself…"

She continues, "The vision takes practice for sure, because we move in so much disbelief, ignoring our own instincts, because maybe it's not a comfortable feeling or we don't want to think that way, we don't want to believe that way, or whatever.

"But I think now [about] where I've gotten in my life, because I've been through so much that

I've had so much practice at just taking those leaps of faith and trusting my vision.

"I know that I have made a hundred thousand mistakes—I don't even know how many mistakes I've made in my entire life—and I will continue to make those mistakes, but I look back, and I see the beauty that came out of a lot of those mistakes.

"Don't get me wrong. Some of those mistakes I could have done without. I'm not proud of all of them, but I'm still okay."

I tell Jeremie, "I think both Debra Jean's and Ragga Surf Cafe are in many ways the inspiration for this book…and also The Inlet. I feel deeply connected to all three of you guys. There's like a vibration. It's like there's just…this love coming out of it all," I say.

Jeremie agrees, "I think you're right. I think it's love. Love is the highest vibration there is. One of our assistant managers, Michael, who won't be here forever because, you know, his dad wants him to go off and make something of his life," she smiles and playfully rolls her eyes.

"But he just loves it here so much that you can see he's conflicted, you know? He's like, 'I just always want to stay, at some capacity.' I say, 'You will. You'll always be a part of this place.'

"Everything that we do, we put love into it. It's not about the money, because that would be a very bad business decision. This is not about the money. This is purely about love. We love what we're doing. We love the Lord with all our heart. We put a lot of love in our ingredients. I take a lot of care to make sure what I'm giving to people is not going to harm their bodies or their minds."

"Did you grow up in The Hammock?" I ask.

"I did. Yeah. I moved to The Hammock when I was twelve years old. We used to ride our dirt bikes and four-wheelers and play 'manhunt' where all these communities now are. So…it's very different now.

"I've always felt home here in The Hammock. I moved away for a little bit and bought a different house. I was only there eighteen months. It did not feel right. It's like I was missing a limb! I needed to be back home."

Jeremie continues, "I try to be a light. If people really knew my story and knew where I came from…" She pauses. "I had nothing. People so easily come in here and judge that I must be rolling in it. We're not. Like, this was an inch-by-inch, struggle-by-struggle, penny-by-penny thing. And it still is on some days. It wasn't that long ago where I was a single mom and I couldn't even buy a home. That wasn't that long ago. So the fact that I own a home and own a business [is a big deal]. I haven't had anything handed to me. It's all been by the grace of God."

We begin talking a bit about politics but less about the opposing perspectives and more about how we can be good people, honoring everyone's perspectives.

Jeremie tells me, "I've gotten some flak from Christians in here because I've hired a gay barista. That just disgusts me and breaks my heart, because we're not judges of anybody *and* she's a phenomenal barista.

"That just annoys me and pisses me off. That's what gives Christians a bad name. That's not Christianity, just so you know. That's law and religion. I'm no one's judge. We have *one* judge…That's the stuff that absolutely annoys me. I'm not ashamed of my faith, but I also respect everybody else's beliefs."

As we talk, Jeremie notices two women outside approaching the cafe. They peer in the window, looking like they really want to come in.

"Oh, these poor ladies," Jeremie says. She stands up from her seat, opens the door, and says to the curious women, "Sorry, we're closed today. But would you like to take a peek inside?"

As many people do when they first enter Debra Jean's, they both "ooh and ahh" over the interior design. "Oh! It's so cute!" one of the women says.

Jeremie laughs and turns to me. "See! *If it's cute, they will come.* Thank you, ladies. We open up on Wednesday."

After returning to her seat, Jeremie tells me, "I feel so bad. We're trying to get open on Mondays. We're trying.[2]"

Wrapping up the conversation, I ask Jeremie, "So what's your life goal?"

"My life goal? I have no idea."

We both laugh.

"I'm just trying to get through today. I have such a big vision for this place. I really envision this as a destination spot. I try not to think too much about it, because my brain is so small [compared to] what it ends up being. Even my staff is phenomenal. I couldn't do this without them. I just am so excited. That's the part that kills me, because I just want to snap my fingers and have it all done."

---

[2] As of September of 2024, Debra Jean's is open Mondays!

Debra Jean's Organic Coffee Café
5927 N Oceanshore Blvd (A1A)
Palm Coast, Florida 32137
386 264-6421

Wanda Lee & Destini Wilson
Flagler Beach, Florida

The Old Roads

Tonight I sit with two friends who have known each other over forty years. They've lived in the Flagler Beach area since the 1980s.

Wanda Lee's back yard is a Florida dream. With a wide porch and a lawn that reaches out into the marshland connecting to the Intracoastal, it's easy to melt into the surroundings. Overhead, the thick branches of old oaks reach outward like strong arms above us.

Destini, Wanda's friend, is an old hippie, with crazy stories of her youthful adventures in the 1960s and '70s. I love her grounded yet ephemeral presence.

I met Destini and Wanda several years ago after a hurricane. I was walking along the beach near Jungle Hut, enjoying all the shells and interesting trash that had washed up on the beach, when I came across these two beautiful women in their late sixties.

They, too, were scouring for shells that had washed up in the big storm. When we talked, I found out Wanda was a photographer and Destini a yoga teacher. We talked for a long time that day and exchanged phone numbers.

As the sun sets this evening and the hot summer air cools, we listen to the distant call of crows and watch the display of far-off lightning in the sky. Wanda and Destini have prepared a spread of food for us. We sip iced tea and talk while nibbling on their little delights. The mood is calm, relaxed, yet playful.

"Is it low tide right now?" I ask.

"The tide's coming in. We're having a super-low tide this week. It happens, like, at least once a summer," Wanda says. "You get this dead low. Sometimes it will just be mud flats.".

"Can you kayak from here?" I ask.

"Oh yeah," Wanda says.

Destini chuckles. "Yeah, we've got stories."

"Do tell," I say.

"We both like doing artistic kinds of things," Destini says. "Before all those huge houses [went in on the other side of the Intracoastal], there was so much beautiful cedar driftwood. So Wanda called me up one day and asked if I wanted to go and collect driftwood, and we went out. And then we decided we were going to go to one little island and have a picnic first…or was it on our way back?" she asks Wanda.

"I don't know. I don't remember this yet," Wanda says with a laugh.

Destini continues, "So we loaded…loaded…*loaded* the canoe up with really cool driftwood."

Remembering the story now, Wanda chimes in, "Yeah, *really* big pieces of driftwood."

"Remember that really cool trunk of a palm tree? It was all gnarly and covered in barnacles," Destini says to Wanda. "I hopped on the island, and I mean, it was really hard to get out because it was in the ground, but I'm like, 'I'm not leaving without this!' And I got it out. It was very heavy."

Destini continues, "And then we stopped and had lunch on the island, but we didn't realize that it was an outgoing tide. So [our canoe] was weighed down with all our stuff. *But* we weren't going to give up any of our driftwood."

We all start laughing.

"And we were like 'uhhhhh!'" Destini says, pantomiming paddling as hard as she can. "We had to really dig in to get out. I think one of us had to get out and push, at times."

Wanda adds, "There were a lot of oyster beds out there. There's a little lake called Stomach Lake, before you get to the Intracoastal, and you'd have to watch out for the little oyster beds. You had to navigate around them."

"Are you good at spotting the beds?" I ask, remembering just two weeks ago getting shored up repeatedly on oyster beds I kept accidentally hitting.

"You can tell. The water might be a little bit ripplier, or they might even be visible sticking up out of the water."

"Other times, we'd go out and get Christmas trees. We'd get a little baby cedar. Now there's a whole new development going in right directly west of me. I can see their street lights at night, and there's a few houses already going in. They're going to have houses all along the Intracoastal right where we used to get our driftwood."

"How do you feel about the growth happening around here?"

"Flagler Beach was just a one-light, small town," Destini says. "It was just that one light on A1A…with the drawbridge. I remember Kyle had an ear infection when he was a baby, and the drawbridge was stuck up."

"Oh no!" I say.

"We had to go to the ER. The hospital was in Bunnell at the time. So we had to drive all the way around with this screaming kid with double ear infections, all the way to High Bridge and then backtrack to go to the hospital."

The drawbridge has since been replaced with the iconic Flagler Beach bridge.

"My kids used to get out when the bridge would go up, and we'd run up to watch the sailboat go by, or whatever made the bridge go up. I'd say, 'Okay, everybody out. Let's go.' That was fun. So we saw a big change when the bridge came in," Wanda tells us.

"So tell me about your husband," I say to Wanda. "I heard he was a musician."

"Well…let's see…he was really a great person. He was a singer-songwriter, played mostly banjo and guitar. He played old-time music. We put a CD out. Then we had a band, and we put another CD out with the band. He was from Sanford, Florida. He grew up inland. After we met, we did some traveling before deciding to live in Florida, but I wouldn't live in Sanford because I need to be by the beach. I grew up in New Jersey, so I said, 'If we're going to live in Florida, we're going to live by the beach.' So that's why we went to New Smyrna."

Wanda's husband, known as J.U., was a carpenter who specialized in restoration work. He had constructed several old-style buildings for the living-history museums in the area.

"His company's name was Cracker Construction. The word 'cracker' came from the cowboys and the ranchers who would crack their whips. J.U. was very proud of the name. He was a cracker and a fifth-generation Floridian," Wanda told me.

Upon doing a bit of research, I learned there are multiple ways to define Florida crackers. Coming from the North, I had always been taught that the term "cracker" came from the plantation era with slave owners, but old Floridians have a very different meaning. The original Florida crackers weren't slave holders at all but instead were pioneer settlers and ranchers from Georgia and Alabama who lived off the land. Before the railroads came in, before air conditioning and mosquito control, crackers learned to live in a harsh environment. They had a kind of resiliency and toughness that maybe 'Yankees' at the time didn't really understand.

Wanda continues to lovingly talk about J.U. "He was quite the character. He was an instrument builder and built [our] house, sailed, and built [our] boat. He did everything."

"Did he write any music down?" I ask.

"Oh, she's got a book!" Destini says. "You should go grab it," she says to Wanda.

But before Wanda can get the book, our conversation meanders elsewhere. Wanda begins talking about her photography.

"The marsh art started in the early '80s. I went out on my own in my canoe, when it was real quiet, and I just got still. There was some kind of tree or something [that I was looking at], and I was just spacing out there, and I saw a triangular face."

Wanda had begun noticing the way very still waters would mirror the edges of the bank, causing a perfect symmetry. When one is lying on one's side, these mirrored images often look like faces. So Wanda began photographing them. She now sells her mystical "marsh art" at GOLA, the local Flagler Beach art gallery.

"Nature creates all these really cool faces or images," Wanda says. "I think it dates back to tribal days and when they'd have their ceremonies. They have these masks, and they're all symmetrical. They had to go fishing early in the morning, and it was probably all calm. They had artistic people then, so they probably saw them too."

Destini adds, "I remember Wanda calling me and saying, 'You need to come over. I need to show you something really cool.' I was blown away. I'm like, 'Oh my God, there's *fairies,* and *goblins,* and *aliens,* and all these magical beings!"

"You call them water spirits, right?" Wanda asks Destini.

"Uh-huh."

"I guess that's what they are."

I want to hear more about J.U. and his music, so I turn the conversation back to him.

"So when did your husband pass?" I ask Wanda.

"He passed in 2002, right before my granddaughter was born. He went five years with throat cancer, and then he had a recurrence. But man, we did a whole bunch of stuff. The music here, dancing on the grass. All our music friends came, and everybody took turns on the flatbed truck. Everybody took turns playing music."

J.U. Lee's songs were about Florida, family, and true events that happened in this area. Wanda tells me she played guitar and banjo too.

"They're powerful songs," Wanda says. "I mean, he really was a prolific songwriter."

"Amazing lyrics," Destini chimes in.

"A lot of the people in the folk community that go to the folk festival in Florida really acknowledged his gift for writing songs," Wanda adds.

"So when you say *powerful*, what do you mean?" I ask.

"The words and the meaning behind some of them. I'd ball my eyes out at a few," Destini says.

"'Haitian Lullaby'…and 'The Burning Cross,'" Wanda adds, listing a couple of song names.

"I always cry with that one," Destini says.

"'The Burning Cross' is a song from a childhood memory," Wanda explains. "When he was little, his dad worked with the sheriff's department and would go out at night on patrol and took J.U. with him. He was pretty small. One night, they came across a Ku Klux Klan gathering, with the robes, and flames, and torches. It scared the crap out of him, and he wrote a song about it. I have to give you a book. You'd really be amazed.

"It's written out in notation and chords. I did the book first, and then several years later, I did the double CD with all the songs that are in the book in the same order."

Destini adds, "That was a huge labor of love."

"Before he passed," Wanda continues, "I started to organize his songs, because he would write them on a paper plate…one song was on the back of a program. We used to go to old-time music championships that they had in Florida every year. And this song hit him about the Trilby Depot. That's a really sad one too.

"That song was written—BOOM—all of a sudden, out in the field. There he is with a guitar. I took a picture of him when he was writing the song. [It was written] on the back of the [music championship's] program, all scribbled in. And then he comes back in the camp, and he sings it for me and some friends. All three of us were crying.

"I mean, he sang it with so much emotion. You just feel all this energy coming out of him…and it's like *wow*. That would happen a lot the first time you'd hear one of his songs.

"'Haitian Lullaby' is very powerful too. When the Haitians were fleeing and they were on the rafts, they were washing up all along the coast of Florida."

"Yeah, it was horrendous," Destini says. "So many were capsized. You know, [thinking about] how many people they were fitting on these rafts…the desperation, right?"

"So we had this goofy dog called Founder, named because we found him down on Walter Boardman, actually," Wanda says. "He would take the dog to the beach every morning. And there it was—a raft—right on our beach. It was oil drums welded together. He went down and took a picture of it. It's in the book. That same week, there was a little, tiny newspaper article about the people coming across, and a mother who had lost her baby on the way. The baby died on the way over. She was just so desperate and lost all hope that she just threw herself in the water and that was the end of her too. And so, with that image in his mind and the image of the raft, he came up with the song 'Haitian Lullaby.'"

The three of us become quiet, holding space for the tragedy in the story.

"It's very powerful."

"So I found a picture to go with the song when I could," Wanda said. "His earlier songs included 'Old Dixie Highway'—"

"And 'The Hammock!'" Destini chimes in. "He wrote about The Hammock."

"Wait, what?" I ask excitedly. "He did?"

"I should just go get a book," Wanda says.

"Go get the damn book!" Destini teases.

While Wanda is gone, Destini reveals a little more about Wanda and J.U.

"There was such a deep love and friendship between those two. They were really amazing together. They had so much in common. The music was a huge—a *huge*—bond. They were both such creatives. He was an amazing carpenter and craftsman."

Wanda comes back with the book and a CD. J.U.'s photo is on the front, in his straw hat and thick beard. I gaze at it and feel as if he is there with us.

I ask candidly, "How do you guys deal with hard stuff? I mean, you guys have both lost husbands, and you've both dealt with addiction issues with the people you love. How do you deal with the hard stuff?"

"Well," Wanda begins, "I sit out here. We talked a lot after each of our husbands passed. Or if we're having trouble with a family member, sometimes we talk it out. We offer support.

"Our close friends grieved almost as much as I grieved [when J.U. died]. There would be times when the band would be playing at the folk festival without him. We'd be doing one of his songs, and I'd have to look away. Andy would see me, and he would say, 'I can't look at her right now.' It gets ya'. It's just so right there sometimes. The wave can come at any point. And music, you know, that really connects you, because you're singing his song and you can hear him singing it. We're singing along with him. But after you get that wave, then it's a comfort."

Wanda looks at Destini and asks, "What do you think?"

"Total agreement. That's what friends do. They see each other through births and deaths, and creative journeys."

The sun has almost completely descended over the marsh, and the small sprinkle of rain we had been feeling throughout our conversation begins to come down now in heavier drops. Destini calls her dog, we gather our plates, and we head into the house.

July 19th, 2024

Becky's Journal

Is this the End?

I'm sitting in a booth at Bronx House Pizza. It's early, so I'm the first one here. "All of my Love" by Led Zeppelin is playing on the speakers. I've decided to return here for the closing of this book. However, everything feels a lot less monumental than I had planned for the ending.

I mean, when you end a book, there should be trumpets or trophies or maybe a parade. But instead, it's just me and the massive chicken parmesan sandwich I ordered.

I watched a video yesterday by a young psychologist about the importance of storytelling in our lives. He said we have to—

Oh crap! I just looked at the time. I'm going to be late for work. I gotta run. I guess the story isn't ending with chicken parm!

July 20th, 2024

Becky's Journal

See, this is what happens when you're writing a story in real time. It's hard to find the ending.

I'm up at Bay Drive Beach. It's about 7:00 a.m. I just did the wildest, sweatiest, most powerful dance I have done in a long while.

I want to finish telling you about the young psychologist and his insights about the stories we tell ourselves…

Though we don't always have control over what's happening in the outside world, we do have control over that small inner realm that is ours and ours alone. In our minds and bodies, we get to decide what stories we tell ourselves. We can write internal stories that magnify our failures and perpetuate stories of shame, *OR* we can look for the good and see our errors as tools and signposts along the way. We have that choice.

We have an opportunity to write a tale about our life journey where we, the heroes, learn and grow from our mistakes, emerging from life's tangled jungles with wisdom and riches. We then, if we so choose, get to share all that good stuff we gain with our friends and our community, passing along everything we've learned.

I believe we are at a juncture. It is our time, now, to rewrite the stories, to choose the better path, one where we include not only our own stories but others as well, where we no longer block our own or others' path to joy, where we cease the endless division and instead open to ourselves, to the people, and to our land with a heart full of love.

Two nights ago, I dreamed of a water moccasin. Water moccasins, or cottonmouths, as they're sometimes called, are powerful, very poisonous snakes that live by the rivers all over Florida.

In my dream, this elegant creature was the most beautiful, most powerful snake I had ever seen. She curled and wound her strong body in all sorts of twisty ways, displaying her intricate patterns. I simply looked at her with curiosity and awe. I knew she had no intention of hurting me. She then slithered away underneath an old wooden shed, and the dream went on.

I texted AyoLane in the morning to tell him my dream. He answered me back, saying, "Guardian of the waters. Powerful Medicine. Hook staffs in Native culture represent the connection between the stars and Earth. Now you know a little more about the tattoos on my arms."

Since then, snake-themed synchronicities have poured into my day. So I called my new friend Harmony, who is now back home in Atlanta. I told her about the way snakes were appearing in my life. She just laughed and said, "Change is coming. Big time."

Throughout this book and these fourteen years I've lived along the Florida coastline, I have changed. I have emerged with a new story—a big, beautiful story about connection, about the deeply mythical *and* the very real rivers in my world. A story about strength, about the way the spiritual meets the mundane. A story about the way the rivers always flow, breathing in and out in perpetual metamorphosis.

But I don't think this is just *my* story. It is ours.

As a collective, we are at a precipice. Our skin is shedding, and we are becoming something unfamiliar and new. Where we're going, it's not quite clear. It's a scary thing to let go of the old, but in my new story, change isn't a bad thing. In fact, it's our call to action. This is our next, great adventure.

Through writing this strange little book, I've learned these journeys of metamorphosis should not be done in isolation. As openhearted, curious beings who are also sometimes scared and filled with darkness, we must reach out and connect, because to write a good story, it must include us all.

* * *

This morning, as I headed to the beach, I slipped Wanda's disk into the CD player of my car. Within moments, the sounds of J.U.'s happy guitar filled the small space. Hearing his voice for the first time brightened my heart.

I turned onto A1A and heard him sing these words:

> "I like to travel on the old roads.
> I like the way it makes me feel.
> No destination, just the old roads.
> Somehow it helps me heal."

Somehow it helps me heal. Looks like I've found my ending.

May we all find peace along the old roads…and the new.

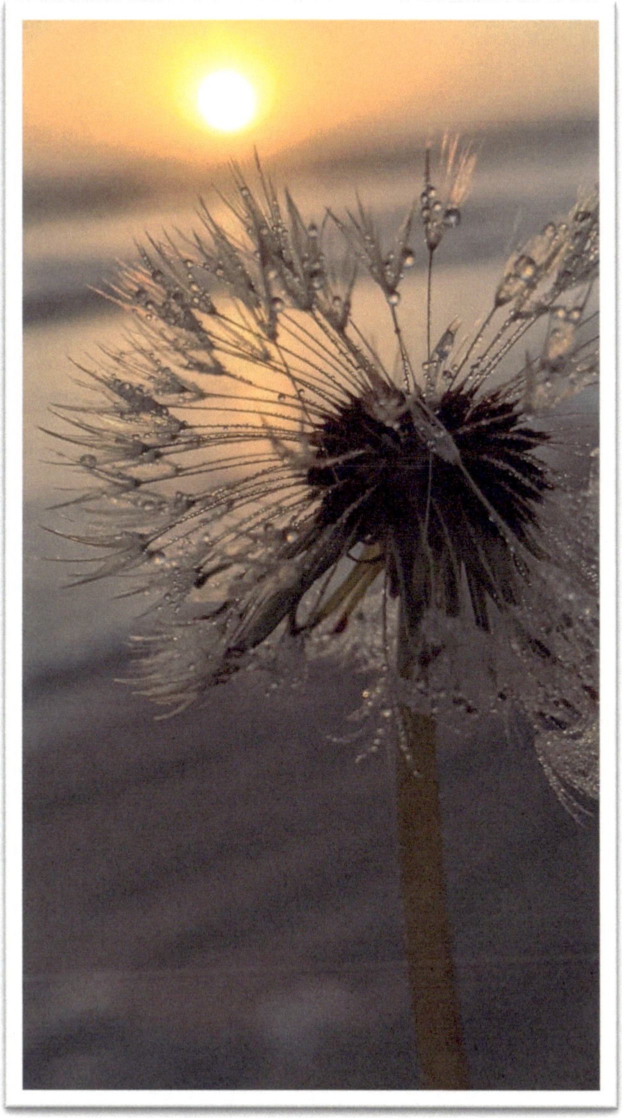

Index of Photographs

Becky and her Dad (March 1972)...3
A1A - The Hammock...8
Becky Magnolia - Matanzas Inlet...10
Mala Compra Greenway Trail...16
Hammock Thrift Shop...18
Becky Magnolia - Jungle Hut Park...20
Randy Odom ...22
Joey and Robin...27
Janine LeBlanc...29
Matanzas Inlet Bridge...31
Jackie and Don Buckingham...32
Jackie, Don Buckingham,
　Becky Magnolia, Don Davis ...39
Becky Magnolia, Audry Scherr...43
Audry Scherr, Don Davis...43
Bob Pickering...44
Bob Pickering...50
Becky Magnolia, Bob Pickering...54
Becky Magnolia...55
Java Joint Staff 2022...57
James Powell...58
Ragga Surf Café...60
Becky Magnolia, Sky (Sandra) Handke
　Hegedus...63
James Powell, Sky (Sandra) Handke
　Hegedus...68
Denise Hagan...69
Denise Hagan...76
Ayolane Halusky - Elkton, FL...81
St. Joe's Walkway - Palm Coast...99
Tovah Janovski...100
Fort Matanzas National Monument...110
Ellen Karp-Bendana...114
Ellen Karp-Bendana...116
Surfside Estate Residents...118
Courtney Alexander...119
Harmony James...123
AyoLane Halusky,
　Darby Brown, Becky Magnolia...128
Jungle Hut Beach...137
Bay Drive Beach...140
Bing's Landing..143
Jeremie Purdy...144
Jungle Hut Beach...153
Wanda Lee, Destini Wilson...154
Wanda Lee, Destini Wilson...160
Butler Beach, FL...169

Made in the USA
Columbia, SC
30 April 2025